# THE OTHER 1%

# THE OTHER 1%

The Story of a Small Family Farm

**DELBERT R. GARRETT JR**

NEW DEGREE PRESS



THE OTHER 1%

*The Story of a Small Family Farm*

ISBN:   978-1-64137-052-3   Paperback
ISBN:   978-1-64137-053-0   Ebook

*Krystyl,*

*It's been years, decades even, since I've written a letter to you. What better place to start again then here? I have so much to say, something about the ebb and flow of time. Something else about love, respect, and children. It is amazing, this power a letter holds. As I looked back over our letters, in which there are many, it is profound how they capture time. It is earth-shattering, their ability to keep two people, teenagers, together over time and space. As was my habit after a letter(sometimes) a poem:*

*Decades--Years*

*Months--Hours*

*Minutes--Seconds*

*Life is in Seconds, The Sun Falls*

*The West in Brief Moments*

*Dusk*

*Beginning--Love*

*Ending--Eternities*

*Love--Time*

*I love you,* **Delbert Garrett**

# CONTENTS

*Farm,*

*I've never written to you. It is something special, the ability to pull someone into your loving embrace, and somehow you have pulled me. We've had our ups and downs, no doubt, but I wanted to let you know I will never let you go. You will have a place in my heart always. Thank you for your brutal reality.*

*Delbert*

*Rest, the peace*

*Soothing, gentle waves*

*Feather breeze*

*Hand of love's entwined*

*Once found*

*Eternity kept*

*Horizon's sight*

*Deep into that darkness peering,*

*long I stood there,*

*wondering,*

*fearing,*

*doubting,*

*dreaming dreams no mortal ever dared to dream before*

# CHAPTER 1

# HELLO

———

In the United States today, 1% of the population are farmers. Of these, only 47.8% farm as a primary occupation. That is 3 tenths of 1%. There are twice as many prisoners in the U.S. than there are primary farmers, in a land of the free where Thomas Jefferson wrote, "Agriculture is our wisest pursuit, because it will in the end contribute most to real wealth, good morals, and happiness." Today, there are more federal employees than farmers. Thomas Jefferson also wrote "The course of history shows that as a government grows, liberty decreases." In the land of the free, it is so sad that so little of us feel freedom.

This freedom is something I get a sense of every day. I am one of the 3 tenths of 1%, I've been farming for 10 years and I am afraid. 2018 is a make-or-break type of year for me and GCC Organics. I've had too many financianaly marginal years for the amount of effort it takes. The struggles of scaling and creating a viable business have been acute. What keeps me up at night is that it is easy for the 99.7% to marginalize something they don't see, understand, or value. I see what value I bring to peoples' lives and hope to bring in the future. To be told by passersby "Why would I spend that much, when I can buy it down the road for a quarter of the price?" is a disheartening revelation in the undervalued

American agricultural system. Blood, sweat, and tears have been poured into my products. I haven't received government kick-backs to help alleviate costs to consumers. I have absorbed all of the environmental costs associated with agriculture instead of passing it down the street for my neighbors to deal with. I have created a picturesque scene that isn't an eye sore and has become a part of a natural system unlike the industrial complexes of most food producers. To these passersby, I say what I produce has value.

By reading this, you will begin to form a connection with the land and people responsible for an important portion of your own well-being.

My story begins on a...

## TUESDAY

### October 24th, 2017

It was a peaceful slumber. Well, almost. I usually forget to drink water until bed time, which means I drink two to three glasses at night. The effect is I need to pee at about 2 am, then again around 6 or 7 in the morning.

My alarm goes off. I'm taking Krystyl to work today, so I'll already be on the Central Michigan University campus for my ENT (entrepreneurship) Publishing meeting at ten. Krystyl starts work at 8:30 a.m., usually arriving a few minutes late, and my plan for the morning is to do homework or farm paperwork until my ENT meeting. What has been nice is that I haven't had to worry about chores in the morning because my brothers, also known as employees/hired hands, will be on the farm to do them. We have cows, broiler chickens, layers (chickens raised just for egg production), and turkeys all out on pasture. We are running broilers— the meat chickens— later than normal because our original estimate of requirements for the year were so low. My father-in-law, Doug, and I have expanded into two new markets, one near East Lansing and the other in Bay City. We didn't know what to expect, and we were pleasantly surprised with the response and need for organic, pasture-raised products. Normally, I like to be done with raising chickens for market by the beginning of October because the weather trends worse for birds on grass, especially in mid-Michigan. This is also the largest amount of turkeys we have ever run. I had ordered 1,500 turkey chicks, poults, to arrive the first of August and, while we only put 1,100 or so into our eight-week range system, from management errors earlier in their lives, I feel confident in their survivability. I've always read that after turkeys reach eight weeks old, they are practically indestructible. This batch of turkeys should push the farm into profitability this year, sorely needed after last year's losses.

As we walk out to the Toyota, I see it's a drizzly morning with water puddles. Colder, too. We had a week of unseasonably warm weather for mid-October. I think one day our high was an incredible 85 or 90 degrees. This colder weather is more what we're used to, but it's a sudden drop. I enjoy drizzle, though, as it always reminds me of childhood in Michigan and of Krystyl in high school. I spent most of my childhood in southern Colorado, where you could always count on sunshine and wind. Having a day or two of rain and drizzle is generally unheard of. My first real connection I had with Krystyl was a walk around her neighborhood in Pueblo on a drizzly day. I smile at the memory to myself as I drop her off at the front of the Bovee Center, the student service center of Central Michigan University. I then park in the faculty lot right next to Grawn Hall, the business college. It is convenient to have a faculty/staff parking permit, with my wife working for the university.

The bottom two floors of Grawn have recently been renovated. I must say that I do enjoy the concept. It includes an open foyer, with glass walls. A sandwich shop was built in, and partitioned workstations added as well. I walk up to the second floor where I will find an open booth. There are only four of them, but at 8:30 a.m. most, if not all, of them will be empty. How many students arrive that early to class?  I take my coat off, pull out my computer, and work on email correspondence, bookkeeping, and school work.

*I wonder when my brothers are going to get chores done,* I think. While I do have them to cover chores, their timelines are usually less than desirable. Generally, I like to get out there first thing in the morning, the main reason being that I want to start my other activities for the day and can't until chores are finished. This is true no matter what I am setting out to accomplish. The reason? Chores are a part of everyday life on the farm because we deal with living animals. They need to be moved, fed, and watered on a daily basis. No matter if my goal is to go to school, go to the park with my kids, or do something around the farm, the chores still need to be done and take priority.

I meet my professor and fellow student in a reserved group room in the entrepreneurship department at ten. We talk about our book outlines, and how our interviews are going. Mine are going pretty well, but I'm not sure the right questions are being asked of my interviewees. At about 10:30 a.m., my phone starts to vibrate. It's my brother, Cameron. I silence the vibration, not wanting to interrupt our meeting by answering. Our publishing meeting wraps up, and we say good bye.

"There are near 400 dead turkeys here. Looks like they piled up," reads the message on my phone from Cameron.

*Fuck!* I think. I call him as I blindly walk to the Toyota. "What do you mean?" I ask him as I start the car.

"I don't know. They are piled up for the most part" Cam is usually so calm. I hear shock and sadness in his voice.

"All in one group or two?" I had decided to split the 1100 into two groups to reduce exposure to risks.

"Both groups have piles of dead turkeys."

"Have you finished chores?" I have to move into action mode. I'm instantly thinking about how we are going to fix this, what has to be done immediately

"We still have hogs and layers to do."

"What the fuck?" I yell out loud. Some kid on a bicycle cycles by in the middle of Bellows and Main, damn near ran him over. There are so many pedestrians and vehicles and now bicyclists. Almost ran the idiot over.

To Cameron I say, "Sorry. Okay, finish those, I'll be home soon. Text Brandon to come over and help."

I hang up the phone as I turn onto Washington. "FUCK, FUCK, FUCK!!!" I yell. As I turn onto High/Remus/M-20, I decide I need to call Fred, founder of a distribution company, Natural Foods. He is purchasing many of this year's turkeys.

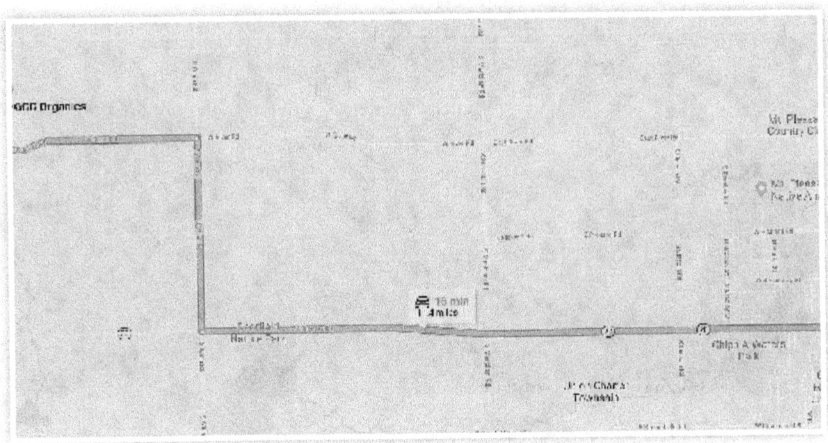

*Route from School to the Farm*

Ring…Ring…Ring… "The person you are trying to reach is unavailable. The mailbox is full…" That's alright. I don't want to leave him a message anyways.

Ring…Ring…Ring… It's Doug. "What's going on? Davis called and said we lost a bunch of turkeys."

"I don't know, heading there now. I'm not sure if this was a predator or weather related. Both groups experienced similar losses, so I don't expect predator."

"Do you think it could be disease, like last year?"

"I really doubt it. Disease loss would follow a bell curve, and we haven't had any losses over the last week. Disease wouldn't hit all to once."

"This will be devastating."

"Yes, and I called Fred but no answer."

"Well, keep me informed."

"Will do, arriving now."

*Overlooking the farm from the hill*

I drive to the house first, which is at the farm on a hill and overlooks much of the 120 acres of property we have in this section. I see my brothers out in the field with a tractor.

I want to run out there and start working on the situation, but I have a problem. I have different clothes for different occasions, much like dress-up Ken. My school clothes are clean and sophisticated. Farm clothes are stained, dirty from the day before, holey, and more importantly, insulated. My shoes have to change as well, from my dress shoes to muck boots, ones which consist of neoprene and rubber. They protect from moisture and go over the foot to just below the knee.

It takes me about 10 minutes to get dressed. I drive out and see the tractor out in the field is the Chalmers. It is our biggest tractor, about 160 horsepower and forty years old. Everything we have on the farm is old, can't afford much else. Really can't even afford the old stuff. It appears the truck is stuck trying to get to the north group of turkeys.

Cameron and Davis are here. "Hey guys, got stuck?" I ask, my breath visible as the drizzle continues to fall.

Cameron answers, "Yeah"

"Okay, let's get it out"

After that, I walk both groups. The turkeys are located in two different fields about a thousand feet apart. One group is in a spring-seeded hay field, the north group, and the other group is in a pasture, the east group. Because the north group is in a new hay field, the ground conditions are pretty bad. Muddy and difficult to drive on with equipment. The east group is in a better field for equipment and mud but the better ground conditions haven't appeared to help the east group either.

*Turkey Locations on the Farm*

There are little piles of turkeys around each whole fenced-in area and then one main pile. It is a massive loss of life and both groups are the same. This surprises me because the field conditions were so different. I can't lament my situation yet. There are still 600 lives in the balance and I must do everything I can to save the remaining turkeys.

Brandon arrives as I finish my initial round.

"Okay, Cameron and Brandon, take the Chalmers and hook onto a hay wagon. Go out and load up the dead. I need a solid count. Any that are still moving that might make it, put into the brooder," I say.

The brooder is a protected house; we raise baby chicks inside. It has heat lamps to keep chicks at the required 90 degrees their first week of life. In these conditions, any weak turkeys may have a chance to survive if we can get them out of the drizzly cold and under some heat.

"What do you want done with them?" Cameron asks, referring to the dead.

"Throw them in the compost pile. Oh, and save me three dead birds from each group so that I can do a necropsy."

"Oh, okay?

"I really don't think this is a disease, but I should check to be sure. Davis, you willing to help me? We need to grind feed; the turkeys are out and the hogs are out."

To help me problem-solve this issue, I reach out to Bob Fredrickson. Twenty years ago, he raised 4,000 turkeys a year and I have a strong relationship with his business. All my feed supplies come from him, and he sells my chicken and eggs. I reach someone in his office and request that Bob call me. As I walk over to get the Minneapolis-Moline tractor and grinder hooked up to grind feed, my phone rings.

"Hello Bob, I've had a substantial loss of turkeys on the farm and was wondering what size of groups you raised turkeys in. My fear is I had too many in a group and they smothered each other"

"When they reached eight weeks, we put all 2,000 -2,500 in the woods together. You see we raised turkeys two different times during the year. How big was your group and where were they?"

"I have two groups of six hundred or so. I have them out on pasture, no real protection from rain or wind. Do you think the woods added substantial protection from these elements, and have you experienced anything like this?"

"No, I wouldn't think the woods added that much protection, but the turkeys always did well in the woods."

"Okay, thank you, Bob. Goodbye."

"Good luck and mm-bye, Delbert"

I see Cameron and Brandon unloading turkeys and walk through the rain to talk to them, leaving the Moline and grinder behind.

Oh, to see the pile of dead turkeys—a rounded mass four feet high and twelve feet long!

As Brandon and Cameron throw them off onto the compost pile I say, "Please try and save any that might possibly make it. After you get done here, we need to move the turkeys. Getting them on fresh ground might help this situation."

It is about 1 o'clock, and the drizzle continues to fall. It's also cold and windy, a terrible combination. Moisture, cold, and wind will kill poultry. When Cameron and Brandon finish the unloading, they head out to the field and get stopped fifty feet in. They look stuck. I see Cameron try to get out and fail. I fire up our little 4-wheel-drive tractor, the Zetor, about thirty horsepower, and head out there with a chain. I see a trench, two feet deep, going northeast and practically fifty feet long. *Fuck, this isn't good,* I think as I try to find a way to the Chalmers that doesn't sink the Zetor. Everything is soft. What do we do? I decide to unhook the wagon from the Chalmers and pull it out backwards with the Zetor... Success!

I tell my brothers, "The Chalmers should be rescued another day; we don't have time to spend figuring out a way to pull it out." As we hook the Zetor to the hay wagon, I point toward the turkeys, "What do we do with these turkeys? We can't even pull a light wagon, let alone drive a grain cart with two-ton of feed on it out here!"

Cameron gestures to the pasture on the other side of the fence. "Why don't we move the turkeys to the other side of the fence?"

"That's a great idea," I reply. "You and Brandon get them moved over there. We will need to leave their shelter." The pasture is ground with a solid root mass that can hold up equipment in these heavy moisture conditions.

"What about their feeder?" Cameron asks.

The feeder is a 1000-to-1500-pound capacity self-feeder on skids. It is a galvanized steel rectangular container with troughs on the two long sides that turkeys can then eat their grain out of. Davis and I are grinding a batch of feed to put in these containers. The feed consists of ground corn or wheat, ground roasted soybeans, fish-meal, aragonite for calcium, and oats.

"It's empty, and though it will suck, I think we'll need to carry it over. With 4 of us, we should be able to handle it." I reply.

Generally, in better conditions, we hook it up to a truck or tractor and drag it to a new location. Because the north group is in such a soft field, we don't have the ability to drive anything up to it. Empty, the feeder weighs about 400 pounds and is bulky and awkward. The only perceivable option is to carry it over a three foot permanent wire fence to the new field.

"Okay" is Cameron's unenthusiastic answer, water dripping down his face from the rain. Wind has started to pick up, and though we are all soaked and cold, the adrenaline keeps us going.

Davis and I head back to the barns to finish grinding feed.

Ring…ring…ring. It's Doug. "How's it going? I haven't heard anything."

"Sorry, been busy trying to save these turkeys."

"No doubt, but I haven't heard what's going on."

"Well, so far the official count is 394 dead turkeys. The Chalmers is stuck in the field, trying to move the north group. We are moving them to the field just south of them. I've called Bob, and he was surprised the birds would smother themselves. I told him I believe it could be the weather and exposure. He said he ran two thousand birds together in the woods and never had any problems."

"What about disease?" Doug asks pensively.

"I still need to do a necropsy to be completely certain, but disease doesn't kill four hundred birds in one night. We will be even more certain over the next few days because a disease will continue to leave the dead behind."

"I feel kind of helpless over here in Bay City, so far away. Good luck."

"It's okay, and we need someone there trying to make money today. Thank you."

With all the questions about cause of death, I decide to do a necropsy sooner rather than later. Cameron and Brandon are back up for tools. I've left the grinder running to mix the feed and decide to examine our sample of dead.

I start the necropsy. Slicing open the lower abdomen to the rib cage, and then carefully splitting the ribs without causing internal organ damage, I splay four dead turkeys open to examine. The birds have a blue complexion, and their organs are saturated with blood. All three of my brothers watch me as I do the necropsy.

"I assume the blood is from being smothered and crushed by other turkeys. Do you see the liver, though? It looks beautiful. No lesions or tumors apparent. Last year, when the turkeys had blackhead, the livers had these yellowish spots on them."

Davis had a suspicion this death may have a disease cause, which I had, by now, almost completely dismissed. "The telling sign for blackhead specifically is the cecum. The cecum is here, and by running it through my hands I feel no firmness in it or any of the intestinal tract." I slice open the intestine. "See, there is no yellow cheese-like substance in here"

"What's that?" Davis asks.

"Looks like a wheat kernel," I say. "I can say that none of these birds have blackhead. The organs, specifically the heart, liver and kidneys, look healthy, so I conclude this was a weather exposure incident."

My driving force this day is to stop other turkeys from dying. I am not wallowing in self-pity because my determination, in this weather, will not allow it. The turkeys need food; I knew this from yesterday. When Davis and I drive out there with the yellow Moline and the feed cart, we carry the self-feeder to the north turkey group. As I drive the cart to the feeder to unload, the turkeys won't move.

"Can you guys help move these turkeys? I don't need to lose anymore by running them over!"

There just isn't any life in them, standing there taking the wind and rain. Some are shivering. Brandon and Cameron haven't moved the east group. They still need to finish the portable fence on this north group.

*2017 Turkeys in Snow*

"Hey guys, I'm going to go get the trailers and use them as shelters," I tell them. It's getting dark, a little earlier than normal because of the solid gray mass in the sky above us. "We won't worry about moving the east group until tomorrow; it'll be too dark soon. Davis, let's go fill the other feeder in the east group."

We get over to the east group and Davis opens the poultry netting so that I can drive in. Even though these turkeys have a shelter, an open v-framed structure with a shade cloth overhead, they are not doing any better.

"I'm going to bring a trailer out here, too. Let's grab those three birds, they don't look very good and we'll put them under the heat lamps in the brooder", I tell Davis.

Doug and I each have cargo trailers we used in the Mission Foods (tortillas, chips, salsa) distribution business in Colorado before we moved to Michigan. I converted mine to a livestock trailer years ago by cutting holes in the front for ventilation. Doug's is still in real nice shape. It won't be after this decision, but I don't know what else to do.

I drop off Doug's trailer with the north group. "Davis, let's move as many turkeys as we can into the trailer."

I help him carry a few into the trailer. Man, they get heavy after a while, weighing approximately 15 pounds. The trailer is south of most turkeys. We try herding them, but to no avail.

"Keep loading them, I'm going to get my trailer to put with the east group."

I get the trailer out to the east group and start putting turkeys in it. I get sixty in there, but I am tired. Even though they won't move around on their own, when we try to grab them they are suddenly full of life. Let me tell you, it gets extremely frustrating chasing animals around you are trying to save. When chicks get out of their portable shelters in the field, a similar frustration happens.

It is an instinctual drive that overwhelms common sense, and you'd rather grab them if only to rip their head off then let them escape. It is difficult to not harm them, when you are just wanting to save them. With the turkeys in this moment, I am too tired and end up giving up.

At the north group, Davis, Brandon, and Cameron have gotten over a hundred turkeys in the trailer, but they are tired, too. Our breaths present themselves in ragged appearances from the cold, and the exertion has made us realize how wet and frigid the conditions are becoming.

"Okay, we did what we could. Let's button up what we can and head back to the house," I sigh.

Brandon goes home, Cameron to the camper, and Davis to his room. Doug is home, after the hour-and-a-half drive from Bay City. During dinner, I tell him what I decided to do with the trailers for shelter.

"Do you think we should go out there this evening to see how they are doing?" Doug asks.

"Yeah, we probably should." I am dead tired, the adrenaline gone. We go out there, but many of the turkeys are not in the trailer. I see the north group is lined up behind the self-feeder, trying to find wind protection. "We need to move these turkeys at least behind the trailer so they have a wind block. They don't move easy, though, and this would be very time consuming."

Doug replies, "Why don't we move the trailer instead?" The drizzle has converted itself to sleet this evening, and Doug's stocking cap collects it, slowly turning the black cap into a whitewashed dome.

"That's a great idea. Gawd damn, it's cold out here!" We move the trailer and then herd the turkeys closer to it.

"I think we need to line bales of straw along the base to stop wind from coming underneath the trailer," Doug suggests.

"It's extra work, and I'm tired, but let's do it." My reply is visible in the glare of the truck headlights.

We do the same thing for the east group: move the trailer and line the side with bales. Some turkeys have escaped the netting to lay down in the tall alfalfa, probably for wind protection. My brothers hadn't gotten to move them today, and that would have helped them.

Our whole management philosophy rests on routine and constant movement of animals over pasture. The turkeys are no different, and had the east group been moved yesterday, they may have survived the conditions better. The north group, with just the seeding of new alfalfa and clover, would not have been afforded the same luxury. Hindsight is 20/20 though and at this point, just speculation. We estimate we saved 600-700 turkeys.

Will and determination drove me through this day. It's 11:30 pm, and I finally lay my head on my pillow. For the first time, I think about what has happened. This catastrophe will have a detrimental impact on this year's bottom line. Will the farm survive this? It will, if I decide it must, but I am so tired. I've dreamed of building an oasis of great food and culture centered around amazing people. The only way to see it is to power through the consequences of this event. I'm just not sure that I can, or that I even have the heart to. As I close my eyes, instead of nightmares centered around cold and death, I pray I dream of happier visions of life and love, perhaps of my children playing in the sun outside, or of going for a walk with my wife in a warm, summer drizzle.

## GOING FORWARD...

This story is the recollection of a journey through time of a small family farm. It showcases the ups and downs associated with humane animal agriculture and farm life. From the joys of raising a family on the farm to the sadness of losing thousands of animals, you will make a connection with the ever-shrinking small family farm and understand the value of keeping these farms viable.

There is a growing segment of the population who cares where their food comes from and who grew it, and this book is for them. 82.3% of households purchase organic goods, and a subsection of this population dares to take a step further and learn more. This story will make you privy to a world full of life, death, and love. From this knowledge, comes a new connection and culture around great food, great people, and great communities. Help me make my vision of the future a reality. With your help, we can power through the difficulties of a small family farm. This farm has been through many changes over its history, and will continue to change as it adapts to differing times. Make yourself a part of the upcoming changes.

# CHAPTER 2

# CHANGE

___

## 1986-1988

My first memories of life weren't on the farm, but actually the suburbs of west Detroit. A neighborhood boy was playing with me and my toy feed grinder. When we left Detroit to move to Colorado, I remember saying goodbye to that boy, probably the only real childhood friend I ever had. I was around four years old. Constantly moving puts strains on developing long-term friendships, and I am an introvert, making the possibility of friendship even more difficult. From my birth in Colorado, to the birth of my brother Brandon in Michigan, then back to Colorado, there were constants in my life: my dad's parents, Charles "Bud" and Mina Garrett, my mom, Shalee Longdo, and the farm. In kindergarten at Sunset Park Elementary in Pueblo, Colorado, I was asked "What do you want to be when you grow up?" I answered "A farmer."

## 1989-1995

The dream of farming persisted throughout my childhood. My grandparents came every summer when school ended for the year to take us to Michigan. They would generally buy my brother and I a new toy tractor to add to our collection. I'd spend hours with those tractors, on my grandparent's carpet. As I got older, my farming games became more complex. I took pretend money from another board game and started a farming bank. I assigned acreage to each room of carpet, and ran appropriate equipment in the correct order of operations to ensure the crop got put in. I ran different crops and would roll a series of dice to determine yield and price. I thought I was being objective, but it seemed success was almost always at hand. As I got older, my games switched to actual farm work with my grandpa, but I still played my farm games on occasion. We cleared nine acres of trees, piling up roots to burn, and picking stone to stack. I helped bale hay and milk cows. My ideal never changed, and it never faltered. My farming dream was built out of love.

## 1996-2001

I was not in line to be the next Garrett farmer. My uncle, John, had control of the farm when I was young. He had three boys who seemed eager enough. Things change, though, and soon my dad had control. It still never connected in me that I could do this thing, farm. When the dairy operation was liquidated, I was 17. I wasn't offered control at the time and never assumed I could ask for it. I went forward with plans to be a computer scientist until securing love was more important. I moved back to Colorado to pursue this love, Krystyl. She was the first girl to show any romantic interest in me. It wasn't until after our marriage did my grandparents make it seem like I could pursue my farming dream with the land in Michigan. Nothing was ever concrete with them though, and no plans made.

## 2002-2006

One of Krystyl and my visits to Michigan while we lived in Colorado was during the Buckley Old Engine Show one year, which Grandpa always attends. It is a week-long event that features old tractors, steam-engines, cider presses, old-time fiddle music, square dancing, and a steam locomotive. Buckley is the third week of August and was always a highlight of my brother, Brandon, and my visits to Michigan. During this visit, Krystyl and I were sitting in my grandparent's camper. Grandpa was having one of his more candid moments, wondering what our plans were.

"You know, if you'd like to farm, you could farm here." Grandpa tells me.

"I would love to farm, grandpa, but I'm not sure I could afford to." I reply.

"As much as I would love to, I can't take it with me." Grandpa states referring to the farm.

"Well, I know, but I am not in line for the land."

"My kids have all got careers and grown kids of their own. What would they want with it?" Grandpa asks rhetorically.

"I know grandpa."

"We can't take it with us." Grandma reiterates. At the time, her dementia was relatively mild. It would soon progress beyond dementia.

I am unconvinced, assuming the risk was too high. I have a comfortable job with The Colorado Department of Transportation. Convincing Krystyl may prove difficult, but at least she is here for this conversation and knows it is a possibility. And we did talk about it before we were married. Well, maybe not about farming, but definitely living out in the country, away from town. For the first time I think maybe, just maybe, I could really be a farmer.

## 2007

It wasn't until my grandpa was admitted to the hospital that I actively pursued the move to Michigan. Will and determination saw me through the challenges to liquidate in Colorado to pursue the love of a childhood dream. The farm and myself were on a path that would include many twists and turns.

## PRE-1900

While the farm was always a constant in my life, it has been through many changes through its life. Change is a fundamental reality of modern agriculture. The interesting aspect of today's environment is that there is room for niche producers to be in farming while not having to bow to the pressures of scale and technology. The industrial revolution had profound impact on the agricultural community, transitioning society away from an agrarian focus. This resulted in a dramatic shift in employment were currently less than 1% of the population consider themselves a farmer. As our culture shifts away from its roots, my farm has persevered.

In 1898, my great-great grandfather Charles moved his son and wife to a property he barely looked at south of Coldwater Lake in central Michigan. Charles was the son of a pastor from the Battle Creek area. The original plan was to spend the season looking for just the right property, but he jumped at the first property he saw. It was a difficult property to begin farming on. It needed to be cleared of trees and consisted of more clay than soil. Despite its flaws, Charles put in the effort to make it the home where my family started here in central Michigan, about one and half miles north of the old town of Two Rivers and half a mile south of Coldwater Lake.

*Great-Great Grandfather Charles M. Garrett herding sheep in Battle Creek 1890's*

*Cora Garrett, Elmer Garrett (6), Charles M. Garrett taken before moving up to Coldwater Lake in 1898.*

## 1925-1945

My great grandfather, Elmer, purchased property in 1920 one mile south of the original homestead that allowed his dad, Charles, to build his retirement home. Charles built this house in 1933; he was 65. Fourteen years later, 1947, my grandpa, Charles, "Bud," named after his grandfather, moved in. He was twenty years old, and newly married. Ten months later, they welcomed their first child, Anita. He ended up with eight more children, totaling four girls and five boys in that order. My father, Delbert, was the youngest.

## 1947-1980'S

In 1949 he and his father built the first barn on the property. Grandpa started farming with six milk cows. He had other livestock as well including hogs and egg layers, chickens raised for the primary purpose of laying eggs. In 1950 electricity was put in on the farm allowing for automatic water. Before then, hand pumping water was the only way to get it. Electricity allowed for modern living with a bathroom replacing the existing walk-in pantry by 1951. Bud followed the agricultural trends of the time though, specifically focusing on dairy production. He also accepted the chemical revolution of herbicides, pesticides, and fertilizers, and purchased modern tractors and machinery. This resulted in not only the survival but the financial success of the farm from the 1960s through the '80s.

*First Barn on the Farm*

## 1990- EARLY 2000S

In the '90s, and early 2000s, my grandpa pursued different avenues of removing himself from the operation. Uncle John, who now lived in the old farm house, took over operations first and the farm continued as before. He upgraded the milking parlor including automatic take-off milkers. These units could sense when the milk was about out of the cow's udder and would pull off the pumps. This made the process of milking more efficient. He accumulated significant debt trying to live a modern life on a farm. Uncle John's family was in flux resulting in him vacating the farm and moving to Nebraska in the pursuit of love. That void was quickly filled by my father in 1995. The farm again continued, debts were paid, but the stress of a modern living grew on my father. The desire for new machinery, new cars, eating out, and other demands of our consumer society were unsustainable at the income the farm generated and eventually the dairy farm was liquidated in 2000. The only thing remaining was the land and buildings.

One fundamental misstep of my family's farm was its stagnation. If our farm was to survive as a modern, with-the-times farm, it needed to expand production and specialization through the '80s, '90s and 2000s. Instead, my predecessors were happy with their existing living, not seeing the changing farm landscape around them. Most large dairies today only control the building and means of production for milk. They don't own the land the feed is grown on, and sometimes they only lease the cows. Our farm never transitioned to such a focused enterprise and it fell behind. The farm is not fully able to provide a 21st century living for a family by doing the same thing over and over again. What do I mean with a 21st century living? A living that includes internet, TV, cell-phone, clothes, and food.

We currently live in a time of extreme specialization. Just driving down the freeway, you see more and more mega-farms where a farm focuses on one or two commodities, mainly corn and soybeans, or on one animal whether that be cattle, hogs, chickens or turkeys. The average farm has been transformed by the industrial revolution not only by the shifting labor force off the farm but also changing the concept of scale, time, and manufacturing. The farms of our past were a haven of diversity, each animal and crop working off each other to convert wastes into products. Now, today's farms represent the industrialization of society. My farm, as run by Uncle John and Dad, tried to do modern farming on a small scale. These attempts included specializing in the commodity dairy market, and after the dairy's liquidation, commodity crop farming. It resulted in a shrunken land base and resentful families. In his prime, my grandpa farmed up to 500 acres, but by 2004 the farm consisted of only 200 acres. Commoditization of our food has resulted in the removal of the least productive and least efficient farms; it has required massive scale to eke out a living. My fear is that it will soon result in our removal.

## 2007-2008

These revelations have taken time for me to understand. I pursued a childhood dream of running the family farm because my grandpa presented the opportunity. I had no idea what I was getting into. When I moved back to Michigan from Colorado in the fall of 2007, I had set aside $3000 to start my farming career. That was what I had after selling our house and tortilla delivery business, paying off the car and settling credit card debt. The first thing I did with this money was purchase a few feeder cattle. I am not sure if that decision was based on pure nostalgia or the idea that I could run a separate enterprise that didn't interfere with my father's existing farm operation. My dad was in control of the cash cropping of our land at the time. By the spring of 2008, it was apparent to my dad that my grandpa had given me priority for management, and Dad pursued other opportunities. I moved into the farm house in August of that year. It was an unceremonious transition, improperly handled by my grandpa. He has never been one for long discussions on serious family concerns.

During the winter and spring of 2007-2008, I ran numbers on the possibilities of a cattle feed-out operation. My numbers made it seem possible to create a living from such an operation, but it would require volume. To build a legitimate business, I felt it was prudent to form a limited liability company and Garrett Cattle Company, LLC was born. I also read Grandpa's magazines *Progressive Farmer*, both new editions and old. While most of the magazine focused on machine technology, shop designs, and efficiencies of scale, small sections mentioned alternative agriculture. There I learned of a program by Allan Savory called Holistic Management. I purchased his book and workbook. This focused my attention on management intensive grazing. It opened the idea that I should be looking not only at the small pieces of the farming puzzle but also the environment as a complete entity. We all have an impact on the environment around us and our management of our small part impacts the larger community. This environment can mean nature, or business, family or society.

## 2009-2011

My first thoughts on managing the farm was to maintain current cropping plans and slowly integrate pasture to be a least cost producer. I was intrigued by a term found in a Progressive Farmer from the mid-90's, LISA. It stood for Low Input, Sustainable Agriculture. What I failed to understand was that our scale never allowed for LISA to result in a sustainable farm income. This occurred to me during a Young Farmer's Conference held by the Michigan Farm Bureau. In February of 2009, the keynote speaker, Dr. Lowell Catlett, spoke about problems in farming today. "Change is tough. And it ain't what we don't know that hurts us. It's what we know that just ain't so, and it can kill you." He emphasized that there are two broad options that exist for agricultural producers today: one is to get big and specialize, and the other is to get small and niche.

When I returned from the conference, I sat down to talk to my grandpa. "I believe that we only have two options to be successful. We either need to leverage all our, which means your, assets, to expand our land base, build storage capabilities and specialize in crop production."

"I don't like the idea of all that debt" Grandpa replied.

"I am not really interested in the idea either. Instead, we could try to stay small and find niche markets for unique farm products. It'll definitely cost less initially, and may allow us to grow the farm relatively debt free," I suggested.

"I don't understand why you feel you can't make a living doing what we've been doing. You just had a very successful year." His unruly eyebrows arched questioningly.

"The commodity market will not remain this high for long," I argued. "The farm has to have the ability to pay for itself, which it doesn't have. I am not going to be given the farm when you die, and need to make enough to pay for it."

"It's your farm, and if you feel that getting unique is what you need to succeed then I'm fine with it." Grandpa folded his hands, his sign the conversation was over.

That was the most encouragement I was going to receive. He didn't truly understand what staying small was all about, and he didn't appreciate the sacrifices needed to succeed in such a market. He still doesn't understand our market, and sometimes I wonder if he appreciates our struggles, but he does see it. I don't blame him for his lack of understanding, because our economic and cultural environment is significantly different from the one he grew up in and raised a family around. While it was the ability to stay out of debt that drove the farm toward it's current path, I have not been able to remain debt free. I've used debt, and debt has used me, to build what this farm is today but the amount of debt amassed is nothing compared to what would have been needed to scale up to specialize in cash crop production. I am not sure a lender would ever assist us if this was the option we chose.

I'm a fast mover when I've made up my mind. I see a clear path to what I want to accomplish. I read Pastured Poultry Profits by Joel Salatin that spring. It was an intriguing LISA concept that markets a high end product direct to consumer: the pastured broiler. This chicken is raised in open-air, open-bottom shelters that are moved daily across pasture or rangeland. For comparison, the vast majority of chickens since the 1960's have been raised in massive, cramped buildings. This raises concerns with disease, and therefore the poultry industry has been a large consumer of pharmaceuticals and antibiotics. The US agriculture industry as a whole was estimated to consume 28 million pounds of antibiotics in 2009 according to the FDA. Joel's system utilized green grass as a detoxifier and intensive management to see them through to butcher size. He claimed the ability to net $20,000 in one year off pastured broilers. This margin was intriguing, and I set out building my first chicken shelter.

The other major conversion happening during this time was my discovery of 100% grass-fed beef. Cattle are herbivores, meaning they eat vegetation. Their digestive system is specifically designed to breakdown grasses. This is a unique ability that takes a massive converter of solar energy, grasslands, and creates a form of energy which humans can digest: meat. Cattle are not designed to digest grains, but instead to systematically graze the grasslands following the seasons. The easiest way to relate is to remember the roaming herds of buffalo that used to populate the Great West. They followed the seasons as they grazed wide swaths up from Texas, into South Dakota and back. Allan Savory's book "Holistic Management" was a key initiator of this thought process, again.

Our society began feeding grain to cattle because our ability to grow grain far surpassed our requirements for it. We needed something to consume the excess and be marketable to consumers in urban centers, thus creating grain-fed beef. Today, massive feedlots are geared toward one purpose: beef production. Grain is the beef's main course.

While I had grown several feeder cattle for the commodity market, I never attained a scale necessary to be successful. I have always been liquid-asset poor, so the conversion to a pasture and 100% grass-fed system was relatively painless. I built my first fence in the summer of 2009 around a 5-acre parcel and began the management-intensive, daily move system for my cows. This entails a regimen of portable fencing, two lines in front, and one line behind. Cattle are always looking to move forward hence, the two lines in front. For pasture health, you put a line behind them so they don't go take a second bite of their favorite grass, weakening it too much and making it less competitive. The spacing of these paddocks, segmented sections of pasture, vary throughout the grazing season depending on the growth cycle of the pasture, and the nutrient requirements of the herd.

The poultry industry has specialized chickens into two primary categories: egg layers and meat chickens. The meat variety, broilers, have been grown to add mass quickly, reaching butcher weight in seven to eight weeks. During the summer of 2010, I raised a small batch of broilers, as Joel Salatin recommended, to showcase to family and friends. I received support from my aunt Sheila with the direction I was taking the farm. She purchased many of the broilers I grew which helped me continue down this path.

With LISA always in the back of my mind, I had the local elevator grind feed from corn I had stored with them. I went to Fredrickson's Organics for Fetrell's Poultry Nutri-Balancer, which Pastured Poultry Profits recommended for a natural mix of minerals, and kelp, a dried seaweed containing a healthy supply of iodine. I had read that feeding kelp to cattle helps supply that vital nutrient as well. I continued expanding these aspects of the operation, growing the cattle herd almost exclusively from inside, and raising a few more chickens, a few more times a year. On the crop side, I had purchased a cultivator to try to limit the need for herbicide, but still used petroleum fertilizer and sold the crops through the commodity market. This slowly expanding adventure into animal agriculture continued through the summer of 2012. It was important to go about changes slowly, and grow market share for direct-to-consumer products through word-of-mouth advertising because of our limited resources. This slow and natural growth allowed for a personable connection with customers. I could remember them and their concerns because there weren't that many. Slow growth not only allowed for a deeper customer connection but also reduced the risks of growing too large too fast. I needed to master the nuances of growing animals naturally to avert disaster.

In the fall of 2012, I heard of an opportunity to rent land just east of us. I talked to the gentleman responsible for that decision, and he stated he'd like to lease to someone who was going to manage the ground organically. I had been asked about going organic from my chicken and beef customers. Organic is an USDA-controlled system that prohibits certain synthetic and natural herbicides, pesticides, and insecticides. It maintains a non-GMO (genetically modified organism) mandate on all crops and animals raised under the certified organic logo. My response to customers was that I might pursue organics in the future but had no plans. Inspections were costly and the premiums for feed inputs would have made raising my chickens extremely expensive. Yet this land manager's request helped nudge me in the organic direction.

He appeared to only want organic products, fearful of the rise in cancer and other health issues within the U.S., telling me stories of him contacting the Department of Natural Resources to voice his concern of eating a deer he shot that had spent the season eating GMO corn and soybeans. These thoughts occurred to him in the year or two before his desire to convert his land to organic. To secure the lease of this land, I drafted a proposal that would have led to his land being certified organic, and a tiered rental rate that would have accounted for the transitional period, three years, from conventional to organic. While he told me his decision wouldn't be made until the first of the year, when I dropped off my proposal in early December he had already agreed to lease to a large conventional farming operation. I never understood his decision. My conclusion was that the money was too great to pass up, and he jumped at the opportunity. He passed a couple years later from cancer, not finding out until it was too late. When I had heard, a year or two after his passing, it was depressing that he had begun to avoid GMO's and pesticides/herbicides in his diet too late. We know so little about the effects of modern food; no one should be judged harshly for trying to hedge his/her bets.

Thanks to my neighbor's original plan to have his land be organic, I had made that intellectual leap to organic production that winter. That psychological barrier was the only thing holding me back, and I decided to pursue organic certification. This was a big moment, because it went against my grandpa's line of thinking and guidance, and I respected my grandpa so much. He had directly helped me to this point, the last four years, and had a large input into what I decided to do year to year. He continues to support the farm, to the best of his ability in his old age, and still supports my decisions. By taking this step, I was moving in a direction he had never been before, and I needed information he did not possess. In addition, it was a higher risk, because the farm would be handling more money. Organics cost more for the producer *and* the consumer. These were huge barriers to cross.

One of my first decisions down this new track was to create an alternate name for my company, GCC Organics, in the spring of 2013. GCC Organics borrowed the first letters from the Garrett Cattle Company, LLC. Most crop land needed three years before certification could be obtained because the land has to be free from synthetic fertilizers for that long. My pastures that I ran my broilers and cattle on could be certified immediately. This meant I could start selling certified organic chicken that year. Beef still had three years to go because the hay they ate was not certified yet.

I made more changes that year. During 2012, I contacted the Michigan Department of Agriculture and Rural Development (MDARD). I knew I wanted to expand my chicken production, and going through the correct channels with a proper license was the only way I wanted to pursue it. After a review with MDARD, I decided the best place for a poultry processing area was the old milk house and parlor. Over the next two years, I invested $20,000 in its conversion. In 2013, I sold $15,000 worth of chicken; in 2014, $21,000.

In July of 2013, I took a job with a local commercial kitchen worktable manufacturer. It demanded 38 hours of my time, during the weekend Friday, Saturday, and Sunday. It was a job that I excelled at and didn't mind doing. I tend to do well, though, in most job settings because I understand things relatively quickly, don't cause a lot of drama, and work efficiently. It was good pay, and resulted in more income than I had seen in a while. The cash from this job was great, and helped me feel like I was participating more in the day to day financial well-being of the household. It did take time away from the farm though, and that was difficult to let go.

## 2014-2015

In the summer of 2013, Krystyl and I decided to truly pursue raising a family. This was quite a step, because we had not tried to stop a pregnancy from happening since 2007. Our journey to get pregnant entailed trips to doctor offices both near and far, and a journey through painful procedures and hormone injections, ending with in-vitro fertilization in January 2014. I did what I could to help Krystyl with the shots she needed for the process. The most challenging aspect for me, and for her, was the day of egg extraction. That day started with a semen sample, and ended with us back home. In between, I ended up on the floor.

I held Krystyl's hand during the operation, and it was intriguing. They had a screen that showed her ovaries through ultrasound, and the doctor used this screen to guide the extraction needle to each egg sac. Each puncture of the egg sac resulted in a spasm of pain for Krystyl, a tightening of her grip on my hand. By the sixth egg, she wanted to be done. I encouraged her, told her how strong she was. By the end, twelve egg sacs later, the procedure was finished. The eggs were harvested, and Krystyl said all that remained was a dull ache. As we walked her bed out of the operating room, I barely made it to her area before I collapsed on the floor as the stress and emotions of the morning overcame me.

The nurses were concerned for me, but I told them I was fine and to make sure Krystyl was comfortable. After an orange juice and some food, I was as good as new.

Three days later we returned to the office. The nurses put Krystyl back on the table she had been on for the extraction, complete with the ultrasound to see into her uterus. They showed us a picture of two groups of bubbles and said these were the embryos they would be implanting. When we looked deeper into the picture, we counted four cells each. It's crazy to think back now and know that was our children's first picture. The doctor came in and very quickly inserted the embryos, and just like that, after all we had been through in trying to have kids, Krystyl was pregnant.

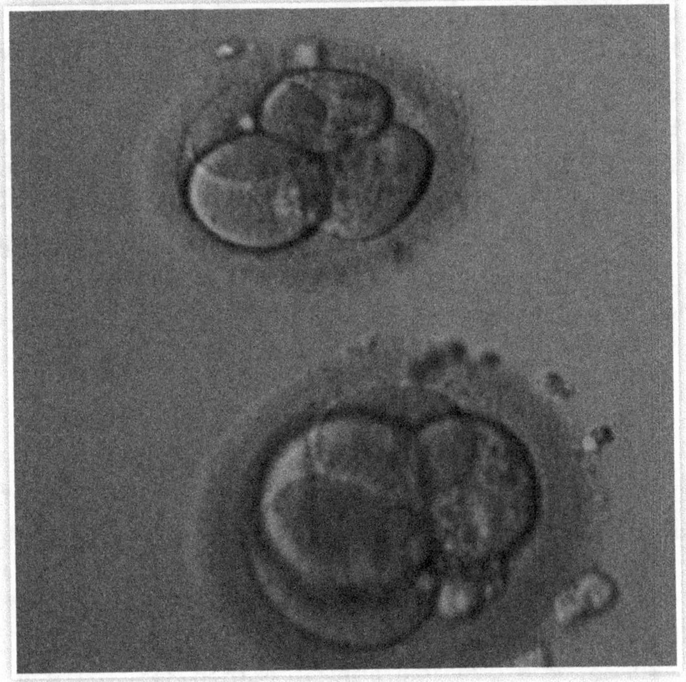

*Rhys and Deitrick*

We had to wait four weeks to return to the doctor's office for an ultrasound to confirm the babies were growing. The doctor only found one heartbeat. The next days were unbearable as we waited for the babies to grow and for the final count. The printout from the ultrasound two weeks later looked like a valentine heart with two heartbeats. We were expecting twins!

The spring and summer of 2014 went quickly. My brother, Cameron, came to help on the farm, which was nice as I was working at the factory. He was never as driven and determined as me, though. His days started around noon, mine started at 4:00 am. When June of 2014 came around, the lack of enthusiasm by Cameron and the ramping up of production on the farm led me to leave the factory.

The pregnancy had been progressing well until August when Krystyl was diagnosed with pre-eclampsia. It required bed rest until the babies were born. Krystyl asked her mother, Jennifer, to come out and help during this time. I didn't mind her bed rest too much, as it meant I got to see more of Krystyl. The situation became scarier when the ultrasound showed that Baby B was growing slower than Baby A. Krystyl's doctor recommended seeing a specialist in Saginaw. Krystyl, Jennifer, and I drove to Saginaw, about 90 miles away.

The specialist's office was on the campus of the hospital. The waiting room was small and felt cramped with stress. The nurse led us back to an examination room and the doctor came in quickly. He used a special ultrasound machine to check on the babies.

"Well," the doctor said, "if you were my patient I'd have you admitted to the hospital immediately. You need to be monitored around the clock. Baby A is sizably larger than Baby B. I'm worried that between your blood pressure and the size difference, you'll need to be ready to deliver very quickly."

"What options do we have?" I asked. Krystyl's fear from the moment of finding out she was having twins was they would have to be born by c-section.

"There's not much we can do other than monitor her and be prepared for the worst. If you were my daughter," he told her, "you would have been in the hospital last week."

We drove back to Mount Pleasant, saw her primary care doctor there, got the necessary paperwork, and drove right back to Saginaw to admit Krystyl to the hospital. Jennifer and I weren't prepared to stay with her. There was a lot to do around the farm, and, as far as we knew, they were just going to monitor Krystyl to make sure she wasn't getting any worse. We expected Krystyl to be there for a couple of weeks.

In the morning, Krystyl called with tears in her voice. "They told me today is going to be their birthday. They told me they won't induce me. I'm going to have c-section tonight at 5:00. I need you here."

I fell to my knees and cried. My boys were going to be born six weeks premature in Saginaw. I very quickly buttoned things up on the farm and flew down the road to my wife.

At 5:23 pm on Friday, September 11, 2014, our lives were changed when Deitrick and Rhys were introduced to the world. They were immediately admitted to the Neonatal Intensive Care Unit. Twenty-five days later we finally took our boys home, along with their prescribed heart monitors. It was a tumultuous and tough time with much of it spent in Saginaw.

*Delbert holding the boys in the NICU*

*Leaving Covenant with Deitrick and Rhys*

My boys changed my focus on the farm. I wanted to be an available dad and a caring father. For the winter and spring months during 2014-2015 and 2015-2016, it was my responsibility to take care of them. It is a time I cherished because it allowed me to become so close to them. With this, the farm needed to adapt to support a larger family. My thought was the only way to build a sustainable family income from the farm was through growth. I continued to forge ahead, deeper and deeper into animal agriculture, less focused on crops.

For perspective, I always felt the best way to grow the business was vertically instead of horizontally. To grow the crop business, you need more land or different markets. Land is expensive, and the different markets could be as well. The amount of space to grow more chickens is relatively small, and I felt that was the best way to go. Through a partnership with Fredrickson's in 2015, I sold $65,000 of chicken. I expanded our product offering with pork during this time as well. I started raising turkeys, too, and egg sales reached $12,000. During the summer, I had help from my brother Cameron and his two good friends. They came with him in early summer from Colorado, and stayed until Thanksgiving. This was a blessing and we accomplished a number of major building projects, including the wood shed, layer house, chicken crates, and the burying of the pasture water system.

*Cameron Ward, Kyle Staples, Ryley Stringer, Delbert Garrett*

*New Laying House*

*Wood Shed*

In October, my wife dressed both the boys, Rhys and Deitrick, in matching shirts that read "This Guy Is Getting Promoted to Big Brother." She was pregnant, naturally this time. It came as quite a shock after our history with problems conceiving. During this time, I realized two main facts: We couldn't afford the daycare for three infants, and I did not have the ability to be everywhere and do everything for the farm. The answer to both concerns took time to develop.

## 2016

For years I had trouble seeing out of my left eye. A condition called keratoconus, a steepening of the cornea into a pimple shape, resulted in difficulty seeing out of my left eye clearly despite every type of lens correction. In January 2016 I had surgery to have a corneal transplant. Krystyl was just finishing the first trimester of her pregnancy, so we asked Jennifer to come help around the house for two weeks while I recovered from the surgery.

The surgery went well and when we were going over the post-op instructions, both Krystyl and I were surprised to learn I could not lift things heavier than five pounds for one month, not one week as we had thought and prepared for. Jennifer was originally going to stay for only two weeks. Luckily, she agreed to change her plans to stay on for a whole month.

I had been thinking about possible solutions to the coming birth of our third child including growing the farm's market share or entering a new industry. During this laid-up period, I drafted two business plans. I flew to Colorado to watch the Super Bowl between Denver and Carolina with Doug, my father-in-law, and present my business plans to him. Through this meeting, I was able to convince Doug to move to Michigan and help me run the farm, with Jennifer helping with the kids during the day.

That spring I decided to expand my knowledge by going back to college. As an employee of the university, Krystyl receives a tuition benefit and she suggested I go back to school as a way to help grow my business. I took her up on her offer and enrolled. The month of May brought busy farm life, preparing for the birth of my third child as Krystyl entered her third trimester, and my first college classes in nearly a decade.

I continued to invest resources to grow the farm, but managed it poorly, partly because I was splitting my time and attention in so many directions. School, daddy duties, and husband duties took me away from the farm more than I realized. 2016 saw drops in sales of chicken, $26,000; the partnership with Fredrickson's changed as their purchases from 2015 maintained them through most of the next year. Fredrickson's had recently gotten out of processing their own poultry, so I bought their old poultry processing equipment and built a new walk-in freezer, 21' x 12', in the area that used to be a holding area for cows waiting to be milked. These changes drastically improved our processing set up, and they were well worth the sacrifices we made to get the equipment. They made processing chickens more efficient and drastically improved our ability to store product, allowing for increased sales.

Throughout the spring and early summer Krystyl researched how to have birth at home, naturally. She wanted to attempt a water birth and found a midwife with experience in that area. Post C-section, most hospitals strongly advise against natural birth in any subsequent pregnancies. While risks may exist, their chance of occurrence is very low, and her C-section and healing made it highly probably that a natural birth would be successful. The baby's due date was July 4th, but the baby had its own ideas. The night of July 14th, Krystyl's water broke and had meconium, a greenish brown substance, in her amniotic fluid resulting from the baby having the first bowl movement within the womb. We met Friday morning with the midwife in town. She suggested we go to the hospital.

Once we were admitted to the hospital, one in which the post-cesarean natural birth policy was very restricted, the attending doctor agreed to give natural birth a try. The baby's heart rate was strong, but Krystyl's contractions were infrequent and weak. They administered pitocin in ever increasing doses throughout the night, and the contractions became more frequent and strong. However, the baby was still not advancing. Early Saturday morning the baby started to show signs of stress from the pitocin, so we elected to turn off the drip. Krystyl and the baby finally rested, but with no end to the birthing in sight. Sunday morning Krystyl's contractions had started back up on their own, but they just weren't quite strong enough, and Krystyl was starting to lose her fight. The doctor administered a little more pitocin to help Krystyl out. This time she didn't need nearly as much of the meds.

"GET THAT BABY OUT!" Krystyl shouted, desperation making her voice throaty and feral.  I held her hand as I watched my baby being born.

One moment my child was just a little black circle, the next she was in the doctor's hands. The doctor looked up at me. "Are you going to say...?"

"We have Charlotte Anne!" I was so much in shock I nearly forgot to announce to Krystyl whether the baby was a girl or a boy.

To close the evening, Krystyl, Charlotte, and I were in the recovery room with Krystyl and I sharing a small glass of wine. She had to pee, and while she was in the bathroom, she couldn't pee and nearly fainted. The nursing staff came in, laid her on the bed, and administered a catheter. The doctor arrived and noticed the womb hadn't begun to clamp down as it should have. They began to extract a horrendous amount of clotted blood from her womb. Everything appeared okay with Krystyl, though, except appearing faint, and I was assured it was natural to have that much blood after three days of labor. The womb began shrinking immediately after it was cleaned. Another scary, non-emergency that may have been an emergency years ago in my grandma's time, another sign of how much everything has changed in the last hundred years. It was the most intense weekend of my life. Being there for the birth was precious and an experience I'll never forget.

Shortly after Charlotte's birth, we got our turkeys for the season. We started out with a thousand birds, the most I'd ever raised. The chicks arrived and we put them in the brooder with high hopes of a profitable year. I was raising the turkeys for Fred from Natural Foods to distribute through his channels. This was a huge year for turkeys, and I was excited to see the results near Thanksgiving.

It was a sunny morning, when I went out to do chores and move turkeys. I had fourteen shelters to move in two groups of seven. In the first shelter, seven dead. Didn't think much of it, next shelter ten dead, next shelter four dead, next shelter six dead, next shelter twelve dead, something isn't right. I had forty five dead spread out through every shelter, and that doesn't happen. I did a necropsy.

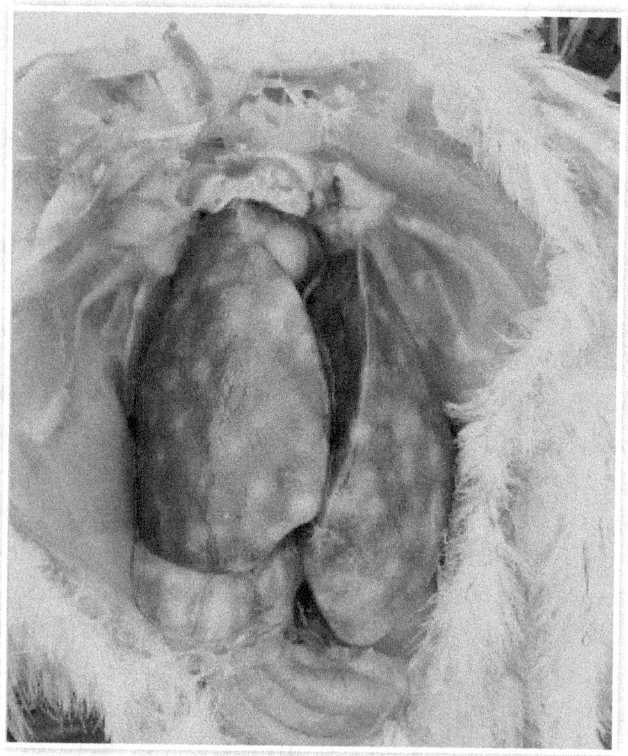

*Turkey Liver with Blackhead*

*Cecum of Infected Turkey*

From what I had read prior on turkeys, it looked like blackhead, a proterozoic worm that enters the cecum of poultry. I reached out to the American Pastured Poultry Association to be certain, and the producer forum agreed. I decided to move the turkeys three times a day, instead of the normal once a day, to get them on fresh ground. The worm tends to spread through the remaining rafter by the eggs dropped in the manure.

The next day, one shelter had three dead, the rest, more than ten each. I tried everything but the death toll rose to ninety one day, and then gradually went back to zero. Our rafter of turkeys was still decimated. We ended the season with just under 300 turkeys, and luckily, Fred forgave the mishap. Despite the losses, we saw a pretty significant increase in sales of turkey. We sold about $15,000. Sales don't mean profit, but one saving grace was that the turkeys were four weeks old, instead of fifteen. They hadn't eaten as much by then.

## 2017

I began 2017 with the same hopes and dreams I begin every season. The struggle of the farm is in the expenses. I have never been able to manage the expenses of operating the business so that I can ensure profit. This plague has continued. I convinced Fred that the problems with turkeys experienced in 2016 wouldn't happen in 2017. He ordered a thousand again and I raised 1500 just to be sure. Our problems with turkeys continued, losing four hundred in the brooder, another five hundred in the field, and another hundred on butcher day. What is devastating is that the losses happened later in the turkeys' lives, after a lot of money had been invested in them.

A new market opened in Bay City and another in Meridian Township, east of Lansing. My father-in-law, Doug, was paramount in pursuing these markets. We also did a massive redesign of our chicken packaging. Through these changes, we sold $54,000 in chicken, $15,000 in eggs, and $23,000 in turkeys. Weather hurt more than just our turkeys. Our crops took quality damage from major rain events in June, making them almost impossible to market. 2017 was a bad year for two families, Doug's and mine, with $27,000 in net loss.

A fundamental change that occurred with the farm's business model during my schooling was a very specific focus on customer relationships. It is imperative that for the farm to survive, it becomes more than just a food production center. There is a culture, and community around food, that has been lost during industrialization and computerization. The new goal of our farm is to be a hub for the interactions necessary to create real relationships for customers to connect with the land, food, and people necessary to provide them with healthy food. I can credit my schooling for helping me to understand this focus. Otherwise, you can buy food anywhere and it'll mean nothing, and it'll taste like nothing, and it'll feel like nothing.

My life and this farm have gone through extreme changes in the drive to survive. Our head isn't above water, and it is possible we may still drown. While my heart has been given fully to this endeavor in pursuit of a five-year-old's dream, it has run out of steam. Will we learn to swim or sink to the abyss of wrecked hopes and dreams? 2018 will be the make-it-or-break-it year because my love for the chase has waned. My only prayer is that the changes I have enacted over the last ten years result in the ability to surf the ocean of this life.

# CHAPTER 3

# FIRST LOVE

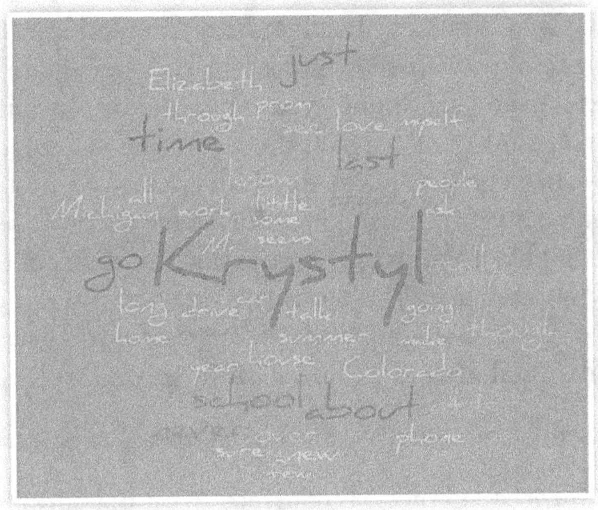

My day starts early with a class at 7:35, and I can't help feeling like I've been here before. But, of course, I have. This is the first day of my junior year of high school, and nothing seems new and exciting. It's the same long and crowded halls I've traversed for the last couple years. The smell of white board markers, chalk, pencil erasers and sweaty sneakers clings to the walls. I've just gotten back to Colorado from my time in Michigan, and it takes an adjustment to live this life. There is an emptiness I can't describe that exudes from this place. Though the halls are crowded with students chatting about summer, I speak to no one. I nod at people I recognize in the halls, but never really establish a connection with any of them. Perhaps work will be better. I recently applied and accepted a position at McDonald's. It'll be nice to have some time away from home and earn money. I'm a little nervous; I don't like new social encounters. My family life has never really encouraged me to make any real friends. I can't blame them, though. I have my brothers and family. They are what's most important. McDonald's won't be so bad because I will be the new kid, I'm quiet, and I like to get involved in my work. Just need to get through my next class, orchestra.

My grandpa gave me my first violin, my fiddle. Grandpa and Grandma always took my brother, Brandon, and me with them to jamborees and square dances over the summer where Grandpa played fiddle and grandma played the keyboard. I would record them playing music and listen to the recordings during the school year. I have been playing fiddle since 6th grade in orchestra. While not the same style of music, I do find enjoyment in playing in orchestra but not enough to devote serious amounts of time to it. I've always wanted to just fiddle around. Mr. Gigliani is my teacher. I've played in the South High School orchestra for the last 2 years. I'll take my usual place in the back of the second violins.

"Krystyl Lentz, go sit next to Mr. Garrett, there," says Mr. Gigliani.

He has always called me "Mr. Garrett." I am not sure if it is just easier than saying Delbert. It's a family name: I'm named after my dad, and he was named for Grandma's uncle. No one outside my family seems to ever get it right. I cringe when some calls me "Dilbert" like the cartoon. But then again, maybe Mr. Gigliani calls me "Mr. Garrett" because of my serious persona.

A skinny blond girl sits next to me, obviously a freshman. It's amazing how young they all look. I suppose I've always felt these experiences don't really matter, meeting new people. This is just a temporary excursion on my way to growing up and getting to where I want to be.

"Hi" She talks first. I guess my head nod wasn't enough. Pretty cute, I must say, but young and naïve. She likes to talk, plays the flute in band, too, I guess. "I haven't played violin long, only about 6 months. I hope you don't mind"

"Not at all." I suppose that's a reasonable response.

As we pull out the music, she asks, "Is that a G?"

*Wow! Really?* I think. "Yes, it is"

As we begin, I find she actually does play decently, even if she is a little unsure of the notes. As class finishes up, I realize how much I really enjoy digging into this music again. Maybe this year won't be so bland after all.

As the months go by, I notice my stand partner is pretty engaging. I must say she is hard to resist. It's Halloween, and she dressed up. I never have, didn't seem necessary. Krystyl decided to dress as Sandy from Grease. Complete with the tight, black leather pants. They definitely caught my attention, as I imagined it did for the vast majority of the guys at school. I'm sure that's the point though, an unnecessary flirtation. She mentions her boyfriend, and I am jealous. Not sure why. I know I would love to have a girlfriend of my own, but my problem is I'm so standoffish. I can imagine interactions where I am the open and friendly one, but I just can't seem to initiate my daydream.

You know what they say practice, practice, practice. I've never really been one for practice, though, violin or otherwise. I don't really want to spend the time on it. At least, that's what I tell myself, and it's true for the violin. The truth for socializing is the thought of practicing makes me break out with cold sweats from fear. In a forced connection, such as sharing a stand in orchestra, the situation creates the time necessary for me to open up, and

Krystyl is so receptive to it. My persona, many times, gives people the opposite response of the one I need.

Thanksgiving is coming up soon. I don't have any special plans, but in the interest of being friendly I think to ask Krystyl. That's when I notice she's got something written on her pants at the top of her knee.

"What does that say?" I ask.

Krystyl blushes lightly. I nearly drop my bow.

"It's just doodles," she says coyly. I can see it's writing, maybe a name? Maybe she can tell I won't let her off the hook so easily. "It's my boyfriend's name."

When did she get a new boyfriend? I thought she just broke up with some guy last week!

"Krystyl, and Mr. Garrett!"

I look up. Mr. Gigliani is looking my way. Perhaps Krystyl and I were talking a little too much. I have never been called out for this type of behavior, and it comes as a shock. I pull my violin to my shoulder, and give Krystyl a smirk. She has a way to talk to me that opens me up more than most. She does a great job of sounding interested in what I have to say. Nothing like last year, with that interview-type question and answer during lunch with Michelle, a girl who was in my English class.

The weather is starting to warm up, and the whole school seems antsy to get outside. Krystyl is no different.

"You should take me out to lunch," she says.

"Why?" I honestly can't think of a reason she would want to go to lunch with me.

"Because you have a car, and we have an open campus, and it would be fun."

She's been bugging me more consistently about taking her off campus for lunch. I am not sure why, though. It doesn't seem very efficient, and I'd rather stay so I don't have to deal with the traffic and time constraints. We all know who wins that battle, but I delay as long as I can. She whittles down my reserves, and I finally agree to take her to lunch. She wants to go to Subway, and since I've never eaten there, it'll be an adventure.

We stand in line, and she orders her sandwich. Now it's my turn… so many choices. *Um, BLT! I know what that is. I'll order that.*

"What type of bread?" says the lady behind the counter.

"Er, wheat?" I say.

"What type of cheese?"

*Um, cheese on a BLT?* "No cheese please"

"What type of vegetables would you like?"

*Let's see B, bacon, L, lettuce, T, tomato, seems pretty straightforward to me.* I didn't want any of the other vegetables.

"I don't need any extra vegetables, thank you" I say.

"Would you like sauce?"

*Well, generally a BLT has mayo, do I have to ask them for it? It's not in the title though…*"Mayo, please".

I pay and go sit with Krystyl. I open my sandwich, bacon and mayo. No lettuce, no tomato. *What is wrong with this place?*

Krystyl laughs at me as I stare confusedly down at my sandwich.

"What? I ordered a BLT, it should at least come with the basics of a BLT without having to tell them what goes on it. I didn't want anything else on it."

"You have to order the vegetables you want on it!," Krystyl laughs.

"Oh." I join her in laughing. What else can I do in this situation? I eat my bacon and mayo sandwich just the same.

I've found myself looking forward to orchestra, and it isn't all from the joy of playing. We are participating in the large group ensemble competition held at the university nearby. It is up to us to get a ride over there, about 20 minutes away. Krystyl and I decide to ride together. We had to run to my house to change first. This is the first time I've had anyone in this house, despite calling it home for the last eight years. Social encounters were never really encouraged in my house. The last time I had anyone over to my house, I was eight. We've moved a few times since then. At the time, we lived on a road next to an open prairie. I always considered it a desert though. Limited rain fall, sage brush, the hard thistle-covered burrs we called stickers, and dirt. I remember three things about that place: playing Karate Kid with my brother Brandon, which ended when I kicked him in the face and his nose bled; the mossy rock fireplace; and having my friend Josh over. He never came over again. I can't recall why.

I put on my dress pants and shirt in my room, while she changes in the bathroom. I've enjoyed her company and our growing friendship over the last few months. It has only taken that long, a few months to create a friendship. This is great for me. Most people would have moved a lot faster....

As we are getting ready to leave, she turns to me and says, "You should take me to prom."

"You just want to be the only freshman there!" I reply. I'm surprised by this request. It's so out of the blue, I don't know how to react. "Besides, I already have a date."

After getting a job at McDonald's, having my own car, and meeting Krystyl, my social network had grown exponentially. I have a friend at work, Alan Paddison. He was going to prom with Dana, who happens to be friends with Krystyl. Alan thought I should go to the prom, too. It was never my idea, but he set up me to go with another coworker, a sophomore named Brandi Worker.

"Who are you taking?" Krystyl asks. Does she look a little hurt?

"Brandi Worker." I say almost sheepishly.

"I know her, and I've heard her talk about parties and stuff. She is just using you to get there, and she's going to ditch you once you get into the dance."

Krystyl is right, of course, but I had given my word to Alan that I would take Brandi before I was really comfortable with Krystyl. This comfort didn't really happen until after she was single, which honestly didn't happen very often. Prom night arrives, and I take Brandi to prom, in her car, and she ditches me. I have to hitch a ride to the school after party. In the end I regret not taking Krystyl, and she won't let me hear the end of it, either.

Junior year seems to end quickly after prom. Finals are next week, and with the tests come shortened school days. Krystyl and I plan to go for a walk after class. The weather is drizzly and cool. Very different weather than the norm for a place like Pueblo. Generally it's dry, windy, and sunny, but this afternoon the weather reminds me of Michigan. I feel like I'm home. We decide to walk around the block. I really have grown fond of her. I can picture taking things further than just a friendship.

We spend a lot of time together that last week of finals. We go to the Nature Center and I hold her hand, the first time I've ever held a girl's hand romantically. We go to the Pueblo Zoo, on another rainy day, too, which is weird or as fate would have it. On another day, we decide to drive to the Pueblo reservoir for something to do and see together. I want to take her everywhere, I want to show her everything, and she's interested in what I have to say and what I want her to see. I'm falling in love. Butterflies in my stomach, isn't this exciting!

Summer is near and I will be heading back to Michigan in two days. Part of me doesn't want to go, that's a new feeling. I'm scared, too, because I may never get to be with Krystyl. She is heading to Lake Powell for a fancy vacation with her family. As we say goodbye, we agree to write to each other over the summer and date when I get back. That's the best I could do. My heart is in Michigan.

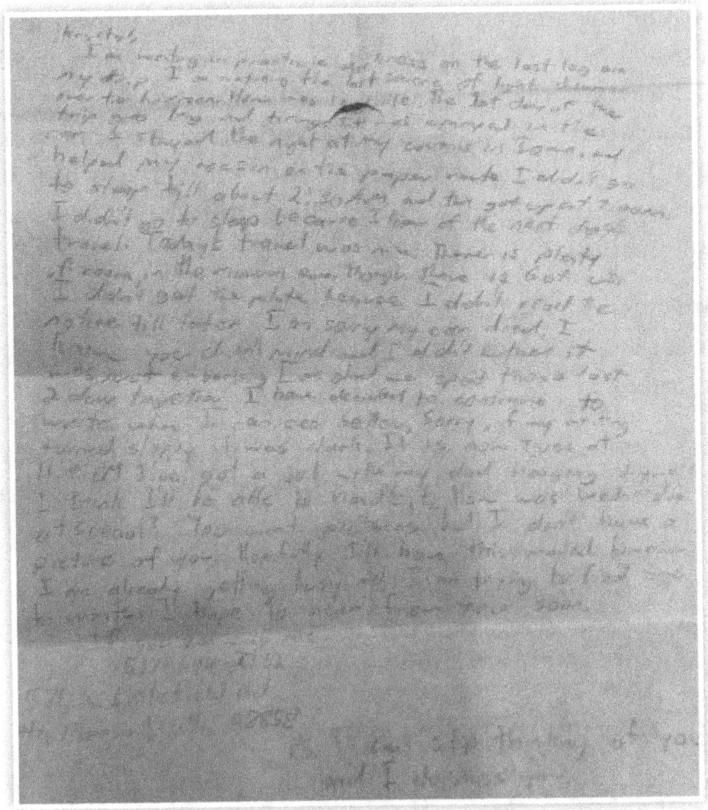

Letters come and go like clockwork. I am nervous when I don't receive one when I think I should, and complain in my letters to Krystyl about not getting more. She doesn't really talk about anything too serious, just what she is up to, and generally describes the events in her life. She sent her driver-permit to me with one letter. Who does that? We talk for three hours on the phone one evening, and my dad and stepmom, Missi, aren't too happy about the long distance phone bill.

That summer, I spend a lot of time helping Grandpa on the farm. We work picking stones, and baling hay. It's hard work, but I love the feeling of strength I have at the end of a long day. I've rekindled an old friendship with Sven. I met him through my cousins, and he is quite the character. My cousins have since moved to Iowa, but he still swings over here. He drives a Dodge Neon and loves the color neon green. I get drunk for the first time, on a six-pack of Zima. I flirt with girls. My dad and Missi are pretty relaxed about my social life— so different from living with my mom. I am pretty happy here, but I'm looking forward to being with Krystyl when I get back to Colorado.

Summer is drawing to a close. Krystyl writes less, and the last letter said we needed to talk. *This can't be good,* I think as I dial her number.

"What's up?" I say. "Are you ready for your birthday party?" The last few letters have been all about her upcoming sixteenth birthday.

"Plans are coming along. We're going to hang out at the lake, just a few of us, and play around on the boat, and then a lot of people are going to head to the bowling alley after."

"Who's going on the boat?" I ask.

"Dana, Marie, Lizzy, Randy," she lists. "And my boyfriend, Joe."

I about drop the phone. We had agreed to officially date when I get back to Colorado. I guess she didn't want to wait that long. I'm startled, but it's okay with me, since I've met an acquaintance of Sven's, Ashly. She seems to be interested in me and my abs. Krystyl makes me feel something special, though, and I know Ashly is definitely a fad. It strengthens the decision I had been wrestling with this summer, to stay in Michigan instead of finishing my high school career in Colorado.

I called my mom last night, and told her I wanted to stay here. She wanted me to know that I was free to make that decision but it wasn't one she supported.  I imagine it'll be the first of many decisions I'll make that my mom won't agree with. This new found freedom has made me want to stay in Michigan, even if I will be leaving behind my brothers. At least I'll get to spend more time with my sisters. In the end, it is a selfish decision and one I will always question because I left behind my family and who I was there in Colorado.

Sven and I have been hanging out more, and girls seem to be interested in me which is a new experience. After I have been given permission to stay, and my dad and Missi have agreed, I receive money from my grandparents to purchase a 1990 Chevy Beretta. It's maroon and sleek, and I feel great driving it. I got a job at a McDonald's in town and after researching a few different area schools, I decide to commute to Mt. Pleasant High School. Krystyl and I stay friendly, still writing letters to each other.

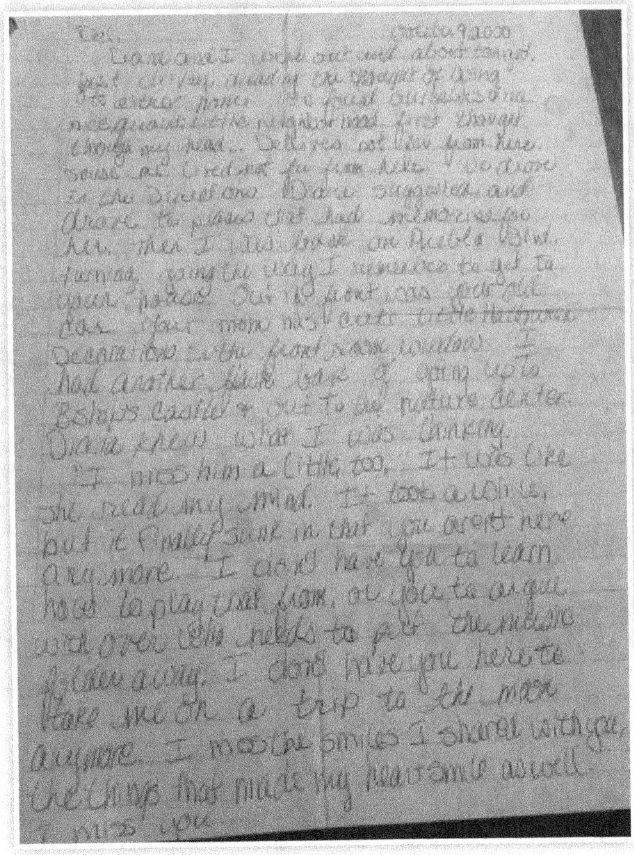

Krystal,                                    10/9/00

    After trying to call you tonight and finding
it unlikely to talk to you, I decided to write
you. It has been awhile so give me a chance.
Thankyou for typing those poems, but after
reading them I realize how horny or stupid
they were. Forgive me. Do you see me
as a loser? keeping in touch even though
I am living 1700 miles away. I was thinking
tonight that if somebody who lived 1700 miles
from me and called what I would think.
Don't they have something better to do then
call me. Do they have no life? That is how
I would think, maybe. I don't want to be
a pain in your ass. Anyway, I have a
girlfriend. Her name is Jacinta. She's a
freshman in college and is very innocent and
straight edge (doesn't drink, sex after marriage).
I tried to take her to homecoming. I rented
a tux she wore a cool dress with black
wings but they wouldn't let us in. I
guess I needed a visitor pass or some dumb
thing. They said they would refund my $24 in
tickets but what about my $80 tux. Those
bastards. I do have to say this school sucks
administration and rules anyways I do talk
to more people then at South though. I do
realize what you mean when you said you
looked next to you and I wasn't there.
I haven't done it but when I thought about
it I was sad. Almost like that person died
and you remember a past moment and you
see that person there and their not there.

when I think about it. I am sorry I
stayed out here. The people I have affected.
You, my mom, my brothers all living their life
without me. It probably affects my mom and
brothers more than you. I do miss them
a lot, enough to make my eyes water. I miss
you too, because you were fun. I haven't
ever talked to Adam. Whatever you were talking
about at the end of your letter I understand
not. I hope that these problems ~~~~ ~~~~ or
held back emotions of some sort figure
themselves out. I would say you could talk
to me but I am 1700 ~~~~ fucking miles
away. You said you can't talk to Diana or
Diana can't talk to you, try talking to your boyfriend.
Maybe he isn't the talking type but give him
a chance to listen to your problems and maybe
he ~~~ can give insight. Hell, you've probly
already figured all this out dy know.
I'm sorry about the tape. It probly meant
more to me then it did to you. Childish
really. I'm sorry I let myself get involved.
Your friend
                Sid

P.S. Analyze yourself, know your feelings, know
    others feelings and perhaps this world will
    turn out a better place.
    Smile only if you want to.
    Express yourself

My senior year in high school goes by fast. I meet a girl, Elizabeth, and we start dating. I met her through a mutual friend at work. She goes to a school west of us, and her parents are strict with her dating decisions. We see each other behind her parents' backs. I always seek approval, so it puts a strain on the relationship from the beginning. We talk about so many things, though, and I feel like I can make it work.

I graduate from Mt. Pleasant High School in early June and go to Colorado for the summer. I work as a laborer for a concrete pipe manufacturer and save up some money. I buy Elizabeth a silver bracelet. I see Krystyl a few times over the summer, but she is very distracted, and she has a new boyfriend. When I get back home, I am ready to start college at Michigan Technological University, MTU, the state's engineering school. It is a very long drive north, about 8 hours. For the most part, I enjoy the drive. The first four hours to Houghton are interstate driving, It's lonely, but I keep myself entertained. The last four hours are state highways that require a little more attention. Damn, that drive is a long commute.  I have a large book of CDs. I can listen to eight CDs on that drive. Staind, Tool, Matchbox Twenty, the City of Angels soundtrack, Mudvayne, these are a sample of my collection.

It is funny how we go through life thinking we have things figured out every step of the way. What is ironic is that most of us don't think about our decisions and how they have a profound impact on others. Even now, it is difficult to gauge my decisions and their impacts. When I was in grade school, probably 3rd or 4th grade, my elementary school, Sunset Park in Pueblo, had built a new computer lab. It had those all-in-one Apple Macintosh computers with the 3.5" floppy drive in the front. The monitor and computer were one unit. A class assignment was to create an animation. Channel 5, the local television station, had a news crew over one day to showcase the computer lab, and my animation and I were featured on the news. Perhaps this was what led to my decision to study computer science. It is something I have an interest in, and it should be an up and coming field.

I am an introvert, but MTU is a lonely place, even for me. When all we want in life is a connection with someone, seclusion can be a depressing thing. I love the weather, though, and all the many feet of snow. I walk the campus at night, contemplating conversations I've had with Elizabeth, the letters I've shared with Krystyl, feeling the loneliness. One of these nights is the first time I think to myself, *I should just step out in front of a vehicle.* The thought shocks me and adds to my depression. I do get to see Elizabeth when I head home but only because she is "sick" on those days. She also tells her parents she's going to see friends when in fact she is coming to see me. What a way to have a relationship....

**

I've been staying in contact with Krystyl through email and occasional phone calls. I haven't put my finger on what it is, but I do thoroughly enjoy talking to her. Possibly because she isn't so serious. I'm serious enough for ten people, and Elizabeth is serious in her own right. It is a pleasure to take a break from all that thinking and drama. Over the winter break, I take a trip to Colorado with Sven. Krystyl goes to the movies with us to *A Beautiful Mind.* She was feeling a little under the weather before we go, and by the time we are done at the theater, she is obviously sick. I say good night and head back toward my mom's when a cell phone rings in the car. Was it intentional that she left her phone in the car? Sven and I drive back to Krystyl's house to give back the phone. When I pass the phone off, I lean in to kiss her. She kisses me back. For me, there is a feeling something electric.

Some time in the fall semester, Krystyl asked me to take her to her junior prom. April arrives and I get on a plane to Colorado. I rent a tux, order a corsage, make dinner reservations. I get to Krystyl's house to pick her up, and I wait by the front door. Her parents' house has a balcony at the top of the stairs and when I see Krystyl as she approaches the stairs my breath catches in my throat. Her black dress and shawl are stunning, and her smile makes my heart skip a beat. We take some pictures in her front yard, and away we go.

Dinner is at Tony's Chop House and goes without a hitch. The dance is at the university, and I'm a little nervous about being with all of those people. Krystyl is outgoing and she's sure to want to dance. She knows everyone here; I know no one. I do my best to let go of myself and have a good time and am surprised when I realize I am actually enjoying myself. We get our picture taken. We dance to Lone Star's "Amazed" and Nat King Cole's "Unforgettable," After the dance we find a moment to be quiet in a park.

"Will you come back to Colorado for summer?" she asks.

"Yah," I reply. "I was planning on it."

"Will we be official?"

"If you can wait that long," I tease. She never seems to be without a boyfriend long, and this isn't the first time she's been asked to wait for me. The last time didn't go so well.

"Okay," she says, "then why don't we make it official now? This will be our first date as a couple."

I'm still technically dating Elizabeth, even if I haven't seen her in at least a month, and our last phone call was a little tense. She wasn't exactly happy I was headed to Colorado to take Krystyl to her prom, even though I explained the longstanding joke of it. I suppose she was right to be uneasy. When I return to school in Michigan, I try to be as honest as possible with Elizabeth, but the truth is I wasn't sure what to expect. That May, after finals, I go to see Elizabeth for the last time. Why I thought I could keep her happy while I was a thousand miles away with another girl, I'll never know. The truth was that was never going to happen, distance doesn't make the heart grow fonder, just lonely and jealous. I don't think I could have kept her happy even if I had never gone.

When I get to Colorado for the summer, my mom and I disagree about boundaries. I've been pretty much on my own for the last year, and I am used to the freedom. She still wants to impose a ten o'clock curfew. I decide to move into an apartment with Alan Paddison. I get a job at the cement plant I had worked at last year, and I add a part-time job at the McDonald's where Krystyl works. We spend a lot of time together, and it causes some issues for her at home, but I'm too much in love to pay it much mind. Near the end of July, Krystyl is over at my apartment when someone bangs violently on the door. Krystyl isn't supposed to be here—my stomach drops. What if it's her father?! Instead it's Krystyl's friends, and they are furious. They drag her away.

The next night at McDonald's I can tell Krystyl has been crying. Alan stops by to visit when I'm on my break. Krystyl takes her break at the same time and comes out to talk to us.

She looks at me through red-rimmed eyes. "Can I move in with you?"

"No. Actually, Alan," she corrects herself, "can I move in with you?"

When she turns to Alan, I know this is not a joke at all, not a try at lightening the mood. Sure enough Krystyl's parents have tired of her sneaking off to see me, and they kick her out of their house. Krystyl moves in with Alan and me, and we start making plans for our future. I am delighted to hear she wants to live out in the country, and she'd like a whole bunch of children. I tell her my pipe dream of moving out to the farm in Michigan, and she agrees it sounds like a good life. Krystyl is a senior in high school and she starts applying for colleges. She puts in her application at Central Michigan University and Adams State College in Colorado, leaving her options open. I will apply wherever she wants to go.

In October, I call up Doug, Krystyl's father, and ask to meet with him and his wife, Jennifer. He agrees. We sit in their living room. I'm so nervous I can hardly speak. I am elated when they give me permission to ask for Krystyl's hand. They even help me plan to surprise her. I arrange for a bed and breakfast in the mountains and pack Krystyl's bag for the weekend. Jennifer helps by taking Krystyl out to lunch, and I meet them at the restaurant. From there, we head to our lodgings in the mountains just west of Colorado Springs on the base of Pikes Peak. Krystyl has never been up there, so we take a drive, hoping to get to the top, but a recent snowfall has the last quarter of the drive blocked. We get out of the car and walk around at the highest check point we are allowed to reach. Her shoes aren't the best as they are slip-ons and she keeps getting snow in them. She is anxious to get back to the car, and I quickly find an exposed rock to kneel on.

"Hey, Love," I call.

"What?" she asks as she spins around. Then I see her breath catch as she sees the ring.

"Will you marry me?" I ask.

"Yes, yes, yes!" She runs back to me, and my heart swells.

My mom is always on the lookout for jobs and sees a listing in the paper for a position with the Colorado Department of Transportation. I apply, not sure what to expect, but I know I need to make sure I can take care of Krystyl. The position is in Alamosa, the same town where Adams State is located, so it feels like a good decision. I get the job and move down to Alamosa in March. Krystyl joins me in May after her graduation. We set a date for our wedding in January 2004.

We have been through so much, Krystyl and I. We grew up together, became adults together. We built a relationship on love. Will and determination kept us connected through the early years of our relationship, just as they would keep us together through the difficult years of our early marriage, just as they keep us strong in our life on the farm. So many years later, I am still in love with my wife and I'm pretty sure she is in love with me. I am a lucky man.

# CHAPTER 4

# WEDNESDAY

---

**NOVEMBER 15, 2017**

The losses of that Tuesday in October were halted as soon as the weather changed and we finally have the turkeys up to butcher weight. The day starts out much the same as any processing day. I get up by 5:30, go over to the processing center first thing, even before my coffee, to fill up the scalders. It is a brisk day, and the steam billows up from the scalders as the tanks fill. The scalders are stainless steel horizontal, half-barrels with a rotating grate attached at each end. After the birds are dead, they go on the grate, and with the flip of a switch, the birds are rotated in and out of water that is kept at 155 degrees. The purpose of this procedure is to loosen the feathers, so they can be removed easily by the plucker. I check the water to the plucker one last time. The plucker is another stainless steel apparatus, a vertical drum with an aggressive spinning action. It is lined with rubber fingers. The freshly scalded birds are put on a spinning plate inside the drum that also has rubber fingers. As the birds spin around, the rubber fingers pull the feathers off. I take another look around. Everything looks set for processing day. I head back to the house for a cup of coffee.

It is hard to estimate how many turkeys we have to process today. We loaded them up last night into two separate trailers, mine and Doug's. His has more turkeys in it than mine, but between the two trailers I figure we have up to 350 birds to butcher today.

We have a newbie joining us today, Carl. He wants to learn about processing poultry, so today he will get his first experience. Cameron, Davis, Brandon, Sven, Krystyl and Jennifer are all lined up to help. Turkey processing days are always all hands on deck. The women will be here when they get here, and my brothers, too. *Must be nice to be sleeping and taking your time getting around,* I think.

Around 7:00 Doug jumps right into morning chores, so I take Carl to the processing center. Man, I'm tired. We had a little trouble getting turkeys loaded last night and we finally finished around 10:30. We were so tired we left the trailer on the truck.

"Help me unhook the trailer?" I ask Carl.

"What's next?" Carl asks

"Er, why don't you get the small freezer in the packaging room emptied into the big freezer? We're going to need to put 200 birds in that front freezer so it's easier for Fred from Natural Foods to pick up. Sven can help you when he gets here. If you finish that before I get back, will you make boxes in the U-Haul?"

While Carl is busy moving product from freezer to freezer, I help Doug with the last of the chores. It's cold today. Sven and Brandon are going to be popsicles by the end of the day, but at least the U-Haul we rented for putting together boxes can double as a refrigerator if we run out of space in the small freezer.

When I finish filling the water tank for the cows, I head back to the processing center and get the other scalder filling. Our hot water tank only holds about thirty gallons, so we have to fill the tanks in batches. We could fill the tanks with cold water and let the propane heat the water, but I find the electric tank to be more efficient, so batches it is.

With the scalder filling, I get the eviscerating tables set up. I look up to see Doug coming in.

"Where's Jennifer?" he asks.

I've been wondering the same thing. "Why don't you text her and find out?" I suggest.

Krystyl isn't here yet, either, but she had to take the kids to town to the babysitter. *How long does it take to drop the kids off?* I think.

The response comes back from Jennifer: she's making dinner in the crock pot. At least we will have something warm to eat when this day is finally finished.

I check my watch. *Shit! It's already 8:30! I've been over here since 7:00. We've got to get this show on the road!*

"Hey, Sven!" I shout to get his attention. He's folding boxes in the U-Haul with Carl. "Get set up, man. Let's get started."

I leave Sven to open the trailer and get started. Joe, Fred's truck driver, calls confused about the weights we gave him from yesterday's processing. I step into the packaging room to walk him through the numbers and finish the call just as Doug comes in.

Doug asks, "Are we rolling yet?"

The processing center is set up as a series of three areas. The first is mostly outside, but under the shelter of the old milking barn. There's a big opening in the side where we have backed the trailer up to the kill station. The kill station is a fairly simple stand built out of 2x4s with cones nailed at chest height. The birds go into the cones head down, and their throats are slit. The birds then bleed out into a gutter which funnels the blood into a bucket for composting. Once the birds are dead, they go into the scalder, then the plucker, and down a chute into the next room, the eviscerating room. Here the birds lose their heads, feet, and guts. The birds are rinsed, then placed in a cold water bath to help them cool quickly before bacteria start to grow. The cold water bath is in the third room, the packaging room. This room has a three compartment sink and two tables for parting and packaging birds, our vacuum sealer, and our scale. The walk-in freezer and refrigerator take up much of the space. I had stepped into this room to take the call from Joe.

At Doug›s question, I look through to the kill station. There are no turkeys in the kill cones. I reply "Shit. No. I don't know what's going on."

I walk up there and the trailer door is down with a massive pile of dead turkeys in the center. As I look into the trailer, Sven is throwing more dead onto this pile.

*Oh fuck...*I berate myself. *Not again. Another mistake, another fucking mistake where minor details were lost, forgotten, or never crossed my mind on these turkeys. And Sven is fucking throwing more and more onto this pile 4 foot high. How many died? Did we put too many turkeys in the trailer?*

*Dead Turkeys*

Doug walks up behind me. "FUCK!"

As with the last time, what can I do? I move on, and I move forward. I focus on the ones I still have. I have no other choice. Doug goes to check on the birds in my trailer. Thankfully, they are fine.

I hear the loader tractor running in the distance. Cameron is bringing it around because we need to clear out the dead so we can butcher the living. The first count of the dead I had heard from Sven was 65, 66, throwing them out two at a time, 68, 70, 72, 74. After the initial count, I can still see quite a few live ones. Without being able to poke through them all, we think the final count is 76 dead.

Cameron gets the loader in place. He can't get very close with the loader because the trailer is in the way, so we started a morbid bucket brigade of the deceased, throwing them in the loader bucket. After two trips to the compost pile, we have cleared the visible dead from the trailer.

Carl's thoughts are written on his face. He looks a little pale and his eyes are wide. "This isn't normal, is it?" he asks.

"No. No, this isn't normal" I reply. I feel a little lightheaded, almost giddy, and I am slightly amused to wonder if this *is* normal.

I look over to Sven. He says "I had opened the trailer, you had just taken that phone call. Shit, I didn't want to get started until clearing this out. When the trailer door came down there were turkeys three or four deep by the back door with more on top."

After we pull the dead out of the trailer, loader bucket by loader bucket, we get started on processing the turkeys that remain. Krystyl and Jennifer have finally arrived, and the first turkey is dead by 9:30. Generally I bounce around a lot on a processing day, not staying at one station for very long before I move to another area to help keep up the pace. Today will be no different but I start at the eviscerating table with Carl so I can show him what to do.

"So, you think they just didn't have enough air ventilation?" Carl asks.

"I'm pretty sure that's what it was," I answer. I had concluded there was no ventilation inside the trailer when we closed it up the night before with 200 turkeys in it. These turkeys were in Doug's trailer which has a small one foot by one foot vent on the roof and it was closed. Since the birds in my trailer are fine, I think this has to be the the cause, not the cold night before. I had cut two or three elongated holes along the sides of my trailer years ago so I could use it as a livestock trailer. When you see actual livestock trailers they have a lot of airflow. The holes in my trailer look nothing like a normal livestock trailer but it has been sufficient in the past. There also weren't as many in that trailer, but I really think it was the air flow.

What's killing me is that with these turkeys over the last two years, I have lost substantial numbers. I have lost a thousand birds per batch. Last year, I began with 1,300 and ended with about three hundred for market. This year, I started with 1,500 ended up with roughly five hundred for market.

*What the fuck are you doing?* I think to myself. At least last year's losses weren't very old, 4 weeks, so the actual cost was relatively low. We still made a profit on the birds that survived, if just barely. But this year? The two events this year, one at 12 weeks, 400 birds, and then this event at 14 and a half weeks, 76 birds, will definitely put us in the red. I estimate these issues will cost us about $50,000 between the cost of raising them and the lost sales.

I take my frustration out on the birds on the eviscerating table. For most people, this is the worst part of butchering. I've done it long enough that it doesn't bother me anymore. I start with separating the head from the body. With chickens I can generally pull down hard enough on the head that the neck separates on its own at a joint in the spine, but turkeys necks have more muscle which makes yanking the head off next to impossible. I don't like to cut through the bones as that can leave bone shards, so we carefully cut through just the muscles as high up as possible until we can tear the head from the neck. *There's that satisfying break of tendons and tearing of muscles.* The head gets dropped into a waste bucket. Next I cut a hole in the saggy skin at base of the neck so I can loosen the windpipe and the crop, an organ that helps the bird digest grain. I turn the turkey around and remove the feet at the joint, then make an incision under the rib cage, careful not to puncture any of the organs inside. I reach in and loosen the organs. If I'm good, I can get all of them out in one pull, dragging with windpipe and crop through the neck. I separate the liver and heart, toss them over to Krystyl to put in the bucket. Those are the only organ meats we save; the rest go through a hole at the end of the table making a squishy plop as they land in the bucket.

I've been doing this for years, on thousands of birds and I hardly have to think about the moves. All the while I am thinking about those turkeys. *What the hell am I doing? Why can't I figure this shit out?* It's very, very frustrating.

It is a long, long day. We end up slaughtering 294 turkeys. There are two more dead in the trailer we couldn't see until we cleared out the living which means that instead of 372, we butchered only 294 because of the trailer mishap. The icing on the cake was the turkeys average weight. The turkeys came in with an average 13-pound carcass weight. Last year, even with the disease that killed most them, we averaged 18 pounds. The five-pound difference is $17 per bird in lost sales revenue. I had grandiose plans with these turkeys; they were going to bring in $80,000. As we were counting on that income, we borrowed $20,000 from a line of credit over the last four weeks to help us process and package these turkeys, cover other debt, and pay for our feed bill. It was supposed to be a big cash windfall. I was going pay off that line of credit. I was going to pay off Fredrickson's, the folks we bought the feed from.  It would be nice to save a little money, and maybe offer Doug $20,000 to help him build a house. It would be so nice to have fewer people living in my house.  This was supposed to be the start of the turn around on the farm.

We'll be lucky if we are even fucking open next year, to be honest.

So, it's tough, it's frustrating, it's disappointing. Turkeys were going to be an immense success. Supposed to be, anyway. These are the things I think about as I am processing the birds. I tear another head off, rip out another set of organs. Life goes on.

It wears off though, the thoughts. I have my music playing on the radio and I listen to a wide range of music, from Beethoven to Lindsey Stirling, from the Beatles to Slipknot, and from Natalie MacMasters to Death Cab for Cutie. Our conversations and the music get me off those thoughts, and I don't dwell on it. We get through the rest of those turkeys, and that's enough for now.

# CHAPTER 5

# SLEEP

Sleep is a drug. The more you get, the more you want. If you try to limit yourself, there's major side-effects. It is a convenient drug, no FDA warning. Your parents don't warn you about it. But I equate sleep to laziness. In the winter I am lazy, because I can afford to be lazy. Not that I can afford many things, but winter laziness is one of them.

In the summer on the other hand, I am filled with the hope and promise of each day, and I start my day as soon as possible. *Can I function with 5 and 1/2 hours of sleep?* I think. *How about 6?*

I have the resolve to limit myself to that amount, and the reason? Because it allows me the possibility to escape from the distractions of life and get things done. Do I always? No. Sometimes I fail myself and just drink coffee, scroll through my phone, or read the paper in the early morning. Quite selfish acts that no one can judge me for. These possibilities exist in the evening as well, but generally, I am too exhausted to relax. In the winter, though, oh the winter…How I love to try and sleep in.

Why? The exhaustion of the summer, the disappointments of the season have weighed so heavily on me that I just don't have the energy to get up. Honestly, I amaze myself that I have managed to regenerate the last 10 winters enough to do this cycle over again every summer. The shortcomings of this last season may be too much to overcome this year, though, even for me. Here we are, post-Christmas, and I have no resolve to get up.

I look in the mirror, and I don't recognize myself. Perhaps it is the fact that I have spent the last three days sick on the toilet, or maybe its the beer I drank over the day…. This person doesn't look like me. Maybe it's because time has passed me by, decisions made I didn't understand to its full extent, or maybe I just don't feel like my normal self. Usually I am so full of spirit, so full of determination, and now I would rather lay in bed. I don't, but I would rather.

The steroid drop in my eye burns a little, required after my corneal transplant surgery, or at least I know it should. Who am I anymore? The boy who thought will and determination made love turned into this hollow shell of a person with three-day whiskers and hollowed out checks… I should have known with the struggles of being married that will and determination make nothing, but human life is made up of a simple sort of wash, rinse and repeat. I almost lost Krystyl because I became complacent in our relationship. I couldn't will her to love our marriage. It took persistence and the understanding that I could move on without her. She had her own battles to win, and I had to let her battle them. We've all made mistakes in our lives. It is our ability to change ourselves and forgive the mistakes of others that let's us grow and change for the better. Sure, we have, as a species, progressed, but the simple struggles of life still exist in every person.

That's no different here on the farm. Our obstacles may appear different, but in essence they are not. I have willed this farm and livelihood into existence and exist it does, but it is far from perpetual. If I were to put a bullet through my soft tissue, this whole thing would go bottom up, and that isn't what I want. I need something to exist after my existence. Human life folks…I am not special in that regard, and perhaps that is the hardest thing to accept. We all want to be special. But you know what, we are. I am special to my kids, my wife, my parents. Because I am here, and because I was there. Humans adapt and they persevere, that is our nature, so life would go on— no doubt. But I believe no one could look at my children the way I do. It would be a shadow of me, perhaps.

Marriage, though, I don't know. I feel that connection could be regenerated with another, and I believe with the divorce rate as it is, many feel the same way. Will and determination don't make love—but they help keep it going, just as will and determination made this farm but only love can keep it. I love my wife, but I don't love this farm anymore. I have worked the last 10 years and have very little to show for it. I could have kept on with the Department of Transportation in Colorado, had damn near 15 years, 5 away from 50% retirement. I wasn't happy there. So many decisions, always in "the pursuit of happiness." What the fuck is that, really? I left the DOT in pursuit of my childhood dream, and I've failed… I just want to curl up, go to sleep, and wake up to find that dream a reality.

This pursuit of a childhood dream has me asking, will we survive? That's something that has been weighing on my mind a lot, and I don't really have a definitive answer. I got up this morning just going through the motions. My desk is a complete disaster, and it's hard to devote time to organizing it and getting it straightened up. I'm at least two months behind on most account reconciliations. Last night I spent 15, 20 minutes trying to find a check I saw the day before. It was a check for only $5, but it does piss me off that I somehow lost it in my mess on my desk. I was going through QuickBooks, writing a deposit for today and couldn't find the fucking check. Am I just missing it because I'm so tired?

I go to bed, alarm goes off at 6:00 am and I think, *you should get up*, but I don't want to get up. I shut off the snooze. I just shut it off, but even then I'm not in bed but another ten minutes. Then I sit there and think about my day. *Well, I want to make some coffee and maybe I'll go do chores.* But then I remember I have Jordan here today, and I want to give him something to do, and I don't necessarily need to go out there. I get up and get dressed and I go downstairs, go through my desk again. Then I decide to look at my accounts online, and I see the business account. A check hit my account for $1,800 but I was only about $1,700 or so short. So the bank charged me $27 and returned the check back to Eric for the hogs. Hopefully his bank resubmits it. I put together a deposit and then I think, *Man, where's that $5 check?* Still can't find that $5 check. I was going to keep a couple twenties to pay Carl for helping with processing turkeys but instead scrounge together all the cash, practically all the cash I have. I was going to keep a little bit back. I have a hell of a stack of fives and ones. I decide that it all needs to go to the bank so that we can possibly cover that $1800 check. I owe the fuel company practically $700 for diesel. I'll have to scrounge to pay that. I don't know how I'm going to pay. The easy answer is to go see Grandpa again for more money. But it is not what I want. I don't know that it's the correct answer.

## EVENTUALLY HIS MONEY, OR HIS PATIENCE, WILL RUN OUT.

I'd like to run the business a lot more lean than I am now. A lot more controlled. But how do you institute those controls? How do you budget and stick to it? When something comes up, how do you postpone that or avoid it so that you stay on budget? Like today...Davis' fuel pump went out. We had to get it fixed. We need the car. But I don't have $800 to spend on fixing the car. Shit like this pops up all the time. I just can't seem to get ahead. It's wearing me down.

I guess this is something I need to spend a lot of time on, but it's this whole balancing act between my other commitments with school, family, and myself. So will the farm survive? I don't know. We are definitely in a cash crunch right now. I don't know if financing is the answer. I think we're about financed out with refinancing the land contracts to pay off Grandpa, getting Krystyl a new kitchen, paying off credit card debt. I had to tap out what resources I had in that department. I also got a $20,000 operating loan that I quickly maxed out thinking the turkeys would pay it off just as quickly. Fate or mismanagement had something else planned entirely.

I don't know. I feel like we're doing the right things. I do. I feel like we're moving in the right direction.

I don't know the answer.

I always tell myself when I go to borrow money from Grandpa, which I've done on many occasions, that this is a temporary thing and we can get him paid back. I don't know, am I just kidding myself? I might be. I don't know.

It brings tears to my eyes to think that I won't be able to put this together, that I won't be able to figure it out. I don't know what the answer is. My mind is warped, and I don't know. I have a lot of ideas, but to be honest I'm getting tired.

I never thought this would be easy, but I never thought it would be this hard. And I've upped the stakes more by taking this mortgage, inviting my in-laws to move in and help, having them contribute financially to the farm.

One thought is that I need to create weekly controls, weekly budgets, weekly expenses, and estimated cash-flows, too. Part of me feels like I need to balance my books first to get a baseline of wherever we're at and I definitely don't have the time to do that. Not if I ever want to sleep, that is.

Maybe I can make it so that every week is a positive net income. Eventually, if I can cover shortfalls in cash that are coming up, we can make this work. So maybe grandpa is the answer. Maybe he can help cover those little emergencies.

I need to do a better job. I need to do a better job of managing. But another problem besides my commitments with school are my commitments toward production. It's not like I have nothing else going on. I don't have time to do these kinds of managerial things.

Part of my problem is just keeping up with all of it. How do you keep up with all of it? I enjoy being able to do everything or having parts of everything to do. I don't enjoy being the only one who can do it. And yet, I don't think the farm, I know the farm, doesn't make enough money to pay for people to know this stuff.

I did a break-even analysis. Based on incomplete data so take it with a grain of salt. Based on this year to last year's growth, and there was growth, our break-even is $216,000 in sales. And our goal to make $100,000 in profit requires $751,000 in sales. That is a substantial number. Getting to $751,000 in sales is a very substantial number. My fear is fucking up the $751,000 and somehow not making a profit even at that level. As income goes up, expenses tend to follow and there are always things to purchase on the farm, things to improve.

So, the question I continually ask myself is "**Will this farm survive?**" The current answer is "I don't know." With love lacking, only will and determination will keep it. I have resolved that this year will be the last year I work for nothing monetarily. I am tired of working so hard for so little monetary gain. It starts with financial management though, never a strong trait of mine. I am further resolved to manage the business into profitability every month and not just a couple months of the year. I think it can be done, but I need to make enough sales to cover fixed costs. Two things: I am not sure I have the financial fortitude for such drastic change in spending and I am not sure my path is the right one.

I am so tired some days I don't have the energy needed to accomplish the tasks that need accomplished. Instead, I draw on pure determination to put forth a good face, and I do accomplish things. It is such a funk for me though, because I am used to driving my day with such enthusiasm and force. It is the love that creates the will and determination. As I lay my head down every night, it is to regenerate this drive for success. I am tired, but I know that after I lay my head down to sleep, tomorrow will be a new day with its own challenges and its own joys.

# CHAPTER 6

# RESILIENCE

—

re·sil·ience

/rəˈzilyəns/

*noun*

1. the **capacity** to RECOVER QUICKLY from DIFFICULTIES: TOUGHNESS.

2. the **ability** of a substance or object to spring back into shape; elasticity.

The ability to withstand and endure hardships and persevere has been a trademark of my personality. My childhood wasn't exactly stable. My mom moved around a lot when I was little, never really held a job for longer than a year or two while I was growing up. We were poor. Friendships and social interaction weren't encouraged. My parents each got married and had kids with their spouses leaving Brandon and I somewhere in the middle, not fully belonging to either family. Still, I pushed through, got good grades in school, managed to get the girl of my dreams. Even then I had problems to get through with Krystyl. We had a really rough patch around our second anniversary when Krystyl moved out and we almost filed for divorce. Somehow we kept it together, with hard work and honesty, and more than a dozen years later, we have a great thing going. On the farm I didn't let frustration get to me when my dad's dogs killed three of my feeder calves our first winter on the farm. Nor did I let the loss of turkeys to blackhead in 2016 keep me from trying again. After this year, though, I am not sure I can use "resilience" to describe myself anymore because I allowed my cumulative failures to consume me.

Perhaps the word should be interpreted differently though. One thing reiterated in my entrepreneurship classes is to not let failure define you, and to not let a failure go to waste. It is the ability to adapt a business model, discard faulty ideas, and learn from mistakes that make an entrepreneur special. Even if I let the farm fail, I have learned a lot.

Adapt and change, pivot and replace, learn and move on — these all are responses to failure. I don't mean the farm has failed, not yet. I have adapted, changed, pivoted, and replaced, all in the pursuit of success. I have illustrated, briefly, these changes. The struggle, though, is proving the concept that I envision. Closing my eyes, I imagine a time when most Americans were connected to the land, to nature, to life, and to death. Communities and cultures revolved around the agricultural cycle of harvest and the rotation of the seasons. This community was facilitated with great food, camaraderie, and the comfort in sharing the struggle, failures, and successes of everyday life, all centered on the land.

With my eyes wide open, I see that around my farm, every day. My goal is to share that with customers who have similar visions and who want to be re-centered around nature's gifts. There is a growing interest and demand in people to know their food and the farmer responsible for it. More and more want to escape the urban jungle, if only for an afternoon, and experience something real, something natural. The growth of reality TV showcases the loss of the real; my farm connects reality to the tactile function of eating.

Now, close your eyes with me, open your senses that have been clogged by the foul stench of burnt oil, gasoline, and asphalt. Expand the ones that have been muted by the screech of tires, the blaring of horns, or the thump of loud music. Increase the ones that have been shuttered by the glare of artificial light, the opacity of smog, or the clutter on the streets.

Now step out to my farm, and un-mute. You'll hear the wind rustle in the trees, birds talking, a cow's slow and satisfying chomp of fresh grass, and laughter. Unclog and you'll smell a summer breeze, roasted hog. It smells like green and growing. Open your eyes, look down and see a chicken scratching for a worm, look up to a brilliant blue sky, look around and see friends and family gathered nearby for a magnificent feast. This is my vision, my dream, and it is something that I must share with you.

How do we get there? Will and determination keeps the love alive, while the love builds will and determination. I've mentioned before my dwindling love for the farm, but it isn't the lack of love for the vision. That ideal hasn't been reached; therefore, love must build the will and determination to see it through. I need to see the vision come true. I believe in its healing power, its regenerative essence, and its subtle ability to build community.

Resilience is needed to survive as a farmer. With your help, my vision of a culture and community will come true. We, as a society, are beginning to feel the pull of nature and the drive for understanding the food we use to nourish us. Let's take this a step further, and while getting to know your farmer, build a community together. GCC Organics will be offering more opportunities to lay the foundation for community around wholesome food, but it will just be bricks without people here to make it meaningful. While I have focused on turkey troubles, there is always more to the story.

Feel free to head over to one of our events, and experience it for yourself. Resilience is needed to survive as a people. Everyone experiences adversity, and we only continue if we power through.

## THE DESIRE

Success... isn't that all we want? The trouble occurs when you define it. I am not defining my success as owning the world. When I was a child that was my idea of success. Now? I want to build something viable and sustainable that I want to pass on to my kids and that my kids want to inherit. I define success as also building something my whole family wants to be a part of. I know that showing them working 80-hour weeks, never spending any time with them, and being in a generally grumpy mood will never help them want to farm. The potential though, for the farm to fulfill whatever their interest is in, remains very high because there are so many distinct aspects to the business. This is where my resilience forms and builds, from the desire to be successful in this new and indirect way.

I have been smacked in the face multiple times. You'd think I was writing a book about the follies of turkey production. I've hinted at it, my troubles two years ago, with the disease. I haven't even mentioned the smaller batches I've lost. I've already placed two orders for turkeys this year (2018). I may be crazy, but I am determined to make this successful. I have learned a few facts along the way: don't turn the brooder lights off, don't allow turkeys to brood over old layer ground, don't expect eight week turkeys to be bulletproof, and don't load turkeys in a sealed trailer for any length of time. Wish me luck in 2018 that I don't have another hard lesson to learn.

My struggles, and resilience through disappointments show through other scenarios as well. Krystyl and I have been married 14 years. I wasn't sure we would make it to anniversary number three. I could have easily walked away, I was 22. I didn't, though, because

I felt the long-term gain far exceeded the initial loss and hurt feelings. I now peer into the eyes of my kids to know that I made the right decision. I have 14 years of memories, that I wouldn't replace for any amount of gold. My will and determination have always led me to face life's hardships head on. Together, with the help of our families and friends, Krystyl and I have done just that in our marriage.

I mentioned the trials in getting pregnant, and our perseverance towards success. We spent six years not trying to have a baby but also not stopping it. We spent one year, actively trying, including uterus mapping and Clomid. All these ended in failure. Either one of us could have said enough is enough. Instead we pursued in-vitro fertilization. I now have kids I want to be successful for. What I have built on the farm to date is a marvel in my eyes, but I'm not in the clear yet. This is the longest tribulation to date, but when I close my eyes, I see the dream of something magnificent. Close your eyes with me, and understand the will and determination necessary to see it come true. I hope I will see you there with me when I open my eyes.

# CHAPTER 7

# DEPRESSION

———

The sound of the alarm startles me awake. *Another day already. I wonder what's in store for me.* I hear the rhythmic breathing of my wife next to me. It must be nice to sleep in. I throw my legs over the side of the bed and sit up, fumbling for the sweats I was wearing last night. The kids are asleep just across the closet from us and I try to move as quietly as possible so I don't wake them. If I wake them, then it is up to me to take care of them until someone else is up. I don't want that; I hardly have the gumption to take care of myself. The cloud in my head makes it difficult to function, but I must. I know that letting that cloud engulf me would be the end of many good things....

I have many irons in the fire, and that has been true since my move to Michigan. Going to school, running and growing the farm, house remodel, mechanic. I wear many hats. Lately, it has gotten to me. I am depressed, and depression can be a killer if allowed to consume you. These distractions aren't enough to completely envelop me and therefore, I have allowed in the depression. It is a combination of being overwhelmed and stressed, and experiencing failure. A lot of this has been brought on by my own choices. I convinced my in-laws to move to Michigan to help run the farm and my family, with many reasons involved, including the costs of childcare and the realization that I can't do everything on the farm by myself. While there are substantial benefits to this decision, it adds stress not only with how many people are in the house but also with the setbacks on the farm. Now it affects two families. And it was ultimately my decision to go back to school.

Krystyl said to me, "I think you should go back to school. Take marketing, or something like that, that will be helpful on the farm."

"Oh?"

"Well, I'm not using all of my free credits from the university. Seems like a waste. And I think it'd be great for you to learn about marketing and stuff like that. It would be immediately transferable to the farm."

"Hmm, could be a good idea." I thought about it for a little while, but eventually took the plunge. I debated whether to attend half-time, just a few classes as a time, but I'm not really one to do things by half. This decision has come at a cost, too, and it's really had an impact on my time. How do I combat it? Lately I just get my feet moving every day. This allows my mind to be involved in something else and keeps me from dwelling on my concerns. It has worked so far.

**

There are so many ways for a farmer to end his life, purposefully or accidentally. According to the Guardian, the suicide rate of farmers is estimated to be five times higher than the general population. This number can be misleading because there are so many ways to make a suicide on the farm look accidental. This rate is nearly double that of military veterans. Why? Well, from my simple perspective it is because the occupation is lonely, certain aspects of the work tedious, and for many the efforts of your labor are defined by a market that doesn't factor in the work. If you haven't made the leap, I am talking about commodities. My farm spent eight years as strictly a commodity farm. Cash crop, we call it. I was not a part of that operation, and the first thing I did when I moved back to Michigan was bring on cattle. I felt the strongest attribute of any farm is its ability to diversify risk and recycle nutrients. Cash crop farming was the opposite of this idea, not only increasing risk but also using petroleum for fertilization… far from sustainable. While my depression stems from a different base, for many farmers, commoditization might be the cause. High inputs, low outputs, no control.…

I recently read in my personality psychology text book that sometimes our greatest strengths are also our greatest weaknesses. I have a hard time determining when my distractions are combating depression and when they are the culprit. I like to be busy, and my life is a testament to that fact. However, feeling the pressure of "real" deadlines creates a stress that leads to depression. I quoted real because before school, I always created deadlines on the farm. The joy of a farming career is that the only one accountable for meeting a deadline is myself: I am my own judge, jury, and executioner.

The ability to pinpoint each of our unique characteristics is a fundamental requirement in understanding our differing moods and conditions. This is how I try to comprehend my own stress, which is self-imposed. In school I have real deadlines and those must be met to secure a satisfactory grade, which, in my unique case, is an A. It's a self-imposed requirement; I have a drive to be the best I can be, to steal a slogan.  I present the best effort to the professors I report to in a desire to display respect and gratitude for their work. When I commit to something, I try to see it through to completion. It means that I devote what I can to accomplish a task, even sometimes at a cost to my mental well-being and health. As I said before, I'm not one to do things by half.

While my traits and characteristics do pinpoint the reasons why I become depressed, outside circumstances play an important role. I have been farming for 10 years and have very little monetary gain to show for it. When I say very little, I misspoke; I have a mountain of debt to show for it. My underlying goal has been to create a legacy or, to be grand, an empire, that future generations can inherit. Currently, though, the situation is rather bleak. For some perspective, I have an $180,000 land and home note that included money for a kitchen/dining remodel that my wife requested and money to pay off most credit card debt incurred by growing the farm. This note, coupled with the issue of (hopefully) short-term cash shortfalls, profitability questions, and the desire to grow have put the farm in a delicate position. One misstep and the operation will fail. Of all my uncertainty, though, one thing can be certain: I don't need to purchase capital improvements to grow the business for the next year. Primarily because I can't afford to. My concern is I can't afford to pay for market growth. Caught behind the proverbial rock and a hard place, I can't be profitable without substantial market growth and I can't afford to invest in market growth. My current plan is to strictly budget the next 12 months so that every month ekes out a little profit.

Every year I have farmed, a rejuvenation has occurred during the winter months that fuels my drive and determination to grow the next year. Most Americans won't understand the yin and yang of farming. It is an occupation that is extremely difficult and time consuming in late spring, summer, and early fall but then transitions into a relatively laid back situation during the winter. I equate it to the changing seasons which allows nature to recuperate from the growing season to be refreshed for the next one. I just hope this winter revitalizes my spirit enough to make it through the next year.

My fundamental concern is that I am not feeling a rejuvenation, but instead I dread the upcoming season. The reason is because seven of the last ten rejuvenations haven't paid positive dividends in return. I start the season with all the hope contained in a baby chick or wheat seed, and end the season with death, unproductivity, and debt. My ability to be rejuvenated in the winter season has been hampered by requirements outside of farming including school, family, and finances. I want to be clear, these are all things that I love dearly, but the cost has been that I can't devote every ounce of myself to the farm. After 10 years, I don't want to either.

Are we actually going to get out from under the red? Are we going to ever return a fucking profit? I don't know if we ever will. Very, very hard to digest. *What can I do?*

I don't know if this is ever going to be successful. I feel like it has the potential to be successful. Whatever that means, I guess. I don't know.  It really is heartbreaking, when I think about it. It gets at me. I put a lot into this, lots of years to try and be successful at this, this farming thing. I think I've been successful in other areas; I've got a family, children, a loving wife.

Now it's real. We have a mortgage to pay after we convinced a bank to lend us the money to pay off Grandpa. We must make that; must make the mortgage. So, what do I do? I need to look at crops again this year to provide cash and develop profitability. I've driven the farm more and more toward livestock production. I have been unsuccessful in providing profits, but feel this is where the future lies. Are livestock going to be fucking profitable? I just don't know. This is the direction I've driven the farm, into animal production. I never have enjoyed the crop side. I hate mechanic work. It's frustrating as fuck. I don't know.

The potential for success, I guess that describes it…really, huh.

# CHAPTER 8

# TENACITY

---

*Delbert holding "his girlfriend" as Doug would say.*

There is a hen on our farm that will never be butchered or harmed by a human hand. This hen has been through the proverbial ringer, but she is most distinctive for the pastel green eggs she lays. She began her life on the farm as a chick in the spring of 2011. She was part of a flock of 50 birds set to be raised to become egg producers. Our production system consists of a rotational pasture grazing system predicated upon moving livestock across the landscape on a periodic basis, and as close to daily as possible. As soon as the weather was warm enough this flock was moved to the pasture behind the house.

*Dead chickens from fox*

As the chickens moved across the field in a portable shelter with an open bottom, a group of foxes discovered them. Foxes are excellent burrowers, and once a week or so they would dig under the shelter and kill 5-10 hens. This continued for some time, and eventually I turned the shelter around so that I could get them closer to the house for winter and hopefully away from predators as well.

*Dead fox*

At this point, we had probably 25 or so hens left. Hens are naturally tropical birds; through breeding, humans have created breeds that can survive the cold much better, but they still need protection from snow, wind, and rain. To overwinter them, we put the hens in a makeshift shed built out of insulated garage door panels. I planned to raise chicks in the same structure. so I used bales of hay to add insulation to help keep the chicks at the requisite 90 degrees The layers had half the shelter, and a batch of 50 new day old chicks had the other half. I had a heat lamp and heated waterer inside for the chicks.

In February, 2013, I took a trip away from the farm to visit my dad in Texas and go on a golf trip to San Diego with Krystyl's dad, Doug. Krystyl stayed at home with our roommate, Dani. They had the duty of overlooking the farm and my friend, Duke, had daily chores covered. Everything was going pretty smoothly. Krystyl had a work-sponsored event in town  and she took Dani as her date. They ended up meeting with some friends, including Duke and his wife, after the work party. They were having a great time bar-hopping and when the bars closed, there was a group that wanted to keep going. Krystyl invited them over to the house.

We had a nice pool table and bar, so we were set up to entertain with style.

Dani had gotten sick from all the drinking. Krystyl went upstairs to check on Dani when she noticed a strange glow coming from our upstairs bedroom window. She looked through the window to see what was going on and immediately ran down the stairs yelling "The chicken hut is on fire!"

At first, no one really understood what she meant but after repeating herself a couple times everyone went into action. I hadn't stored the garden hoses in the house that winter, so they were all frozen in the yard. The partiers put the frozen hoses in the shower to warm up and formed a bucket brigade. Of the seemingly hundreds of five-gallon pails on the farm, they could only find three or four, and they all seemed to have holes. They had six people handing buckets to one another creating a chain of water from the side of the house to the chicken shed 100 feet away. The majority of the fire was extinguished with the buckets of water. Once the hose was defrosted, they got the rest of the flames quenched.

This is the chicken shelter. Notice the black, visible from the outside. This was where the fire was the hottest, and probably where it started.

All the chicks were dead, but we probably only lost about 5 of the 25 laying chickens who were left after the fox attacks that summer. When I returned home, I decided the laying hens that remained would be left to their own devices to survive the winter. By spring 2012, about 15 birds remained and by the fall only two were left. The rest perished from predators, or exposure, or stupidity. One of the surviving hens from the fire was a black-feathered chicken.

I decided to try my hand again at raising day-old chicks during the winter of 2013, and when they were ready to go outside in the spring of 2013 only one hen from the 2011 group survived: a pretty black hen who lays green eggs. I caught the black hen and put her in with the 2013 layers. As they age, hens lay fewer and fewer eggs, but even though she is seven years old, she still regularly lays a green egg in the height of summer.  It always puts a smile on my face when I see that green egg in the nest.

This hen has been on the farm since the spring of 2011 and she has seen many birds come and go. For a bird who has survived fox attacks, a fire, several winters, predation from being without a coop, the road, and other dangers of life, it is my wish that she live. I have not necessarily protected her from harm but I will also not harm her. This chicken has tenacity.

She is the reason I have faith in what we do. I see her will and determination to live. Though there are many struggles on the farm, I know that the end result is worth it. I've seen it in my marriage, too; I now have three wonderful children only made possible by working through our marital issues. Divorce would have been an easier option, but not one that I would accept. Just as I won't accept failure on this farm, and just as this hen continues to persevere.

# CHAPTER 9

# HOPE

—

Five minutes; doesn't seem so bad. There is an analog clock, three feet in diameter, above my head. The seconds hand clicks away. Three minutes left; wow, how much more scrubbing can I do to my hands? It smells clean in an antiseptic way, a chemical clean. Two minutes left. Oh! They have these picks to clean under the fingernails. Should be a breeze to finish now. Parents and nurses come and go through the double doors as they are buzzed in. Ten seconds; okay, I can rinse. I am excited; I'm going to see my boys, but I feel weird, nervous, an impostor, in this foreign hall. I continue as a stranger.

"How may I help you?" the nurse asks.

She should know. I am wearing the appropriate bracelet, I think.

"Here to see Rhys and Deitrick." I reply.

"Okay. I just recently changed them but you are free to hold them if you like."

I nod my head.

Five minutes feels like a lifetime when I'm washing my hands, but the next fifteen go so fast. I pull Rhys out of the incubator, while Krystyl pulls out Deitrick. So many tubes and wires, it is easy to get tangled up. As I lay Rhys on my chest, Krystyl gently lays Deitrick next to him. All my concerns and worries rest right here on my chest.

Isn't it amazing, how something so simple can change the outlook on life. Every time I peer into the eyes of my children, I remember the innocence of life and what I am fighting for. I want to have something worth passing on to them. This is the love that builds the will and determination.

My childhood dream has come true... I am a <u>farmer</u>! It is amazing when I really consider that. God, do I love what I do! I continue for that love and I hope that my children will develop that love and help the farm grow into something more. That is my hope.

Time has flown since my childhood. Moments that are suspended in time and others that barely are noticed. Time has moved fast since the birth of the boys, including the birth of Charlotte one year and ten months after the boys. I've gone back to college for my bachelors in entrepreneurship, I've had cornea transplant surgery, and my in-laws have moved into our house, making the long trip from Colorado.

It's relatively early on a Sunday in late June, 2017. The whole household has been a little lazy this morning. The adults have all had Irish coffee and kids have had their fair share of milk. Everyone has been stuffed to the gills, eating scrambled eggs with cheese and breakfast sausage that I cooked. We've been persistent in requiring the children use manners. They've picked it up relatively well.

"Daddy," says Deitrick, "can we go see the cows? Please?"

Krystyl is nearby listening. "What does a cow say?"

A chorus of moos ensues from both boys. "Get your boots on so we can go outside," I shout over the cacophony. Getting them out the door is always trying on my patience, but seeing them so excited to hang out on the farm warms my soul. Once the kids are appropriately dressed, I lead the troops outside.

"Can we ride in the wagon, please?" Rhys asks.

"Yes. Make room for Charley."

"Charley Sister Baby can sit over on this side with me," Rhys says to me. He turns to his sister and his voice gets high pitched. "Come here, Charley. Sit next to me."

Once the kids are all settled in, the adventure can begin. We aim for the pigs first. As we approach the road, I stop the wagon. Deitrick immediately yells "No cars!" without even looking.

"Did you look?" I ask him.

He's quite a sarcastic kid, even at two, and he jerks his head from side to side and repeats, "No cars!"

Rhys pipes up, "It's safe, Daddy." Indeed, it is, but it's hard to be too careful on this 55 mile-per-hour road with blind hills as we cross the road.

Our garden is immediately across the road from the house. Davis, my brother, has been the main gardener this year. Cameron, another brother, helps him out a lot, too. Davis is out there now, hoeing the bed of sweet potatoes. This is the best garden we've ever had and I am thankful my brothers have taken it on.

"Wave to Uncle Davy" I say to the kids. Enthusiastic arm waving ensues from the boys. Charley has yet to really figure it out, and she kind of rolls her wrist. She's concentrating so hard she has a little frown. The scene makes me smile.

We approach the pigs and a little pink one squeals as he runs away. They can be so fast! The fence is electrified so I remind the boys to be careful as they clamber out of the wagon. They are still so awkward in their bodies; Rhys nearly kicks his sister in the face as he gets out.

I leave Charley in the wagon, taking care of the pigs is generally quick and getting everyone unloaded and loaded takes more time.

"What are you doing, Dad?" Rhys asks.

"Checking the fence. We need to make sure the battery is still good." I reply as I see two green dots on the indicator. One green dot means the battery needs replaced.

Standing here I take a moment to reflect on the last few years with the hogs. We started out with just three in 2015. I wanted to dial in our set up for raising them before I invested in organic piglets. We kept the meat all for ourselves. That was an awesome year with all the bacon we could eat. One of those pigs we roasted Hawaiian-style in our backyard for the twin's first birthday. That was an amazing party with wonderful people. My mom and Doug and Jennifer flew in for the occasion. That party really inspired me, seeing everyone eating our food, enjoying each other's company. I promised myself I would make that happen more often in the coming years and I've kept that promise. The boys' birthdays have always been big occasions, and Sven got married on the farm in 2016. We did a pig roast for that party, too. Charley's coming first birthday will be another occasion to share in our community around great food.

I snap back to reality and decide to walk over to check the pig waterer. No water comes out of the nipple.

"No water, boys. Let's get loaded back up in the wagon and please be careful with your sister."

Charley starts to cry; the wagon is pretty cramped with three kids. "It's okay Charlotte, we need to squish you over. Rhys, make room for your sister, please."

"Okay, Dad. It's okay Baby Sister Charley." Rhys replies as he pats her on the back.

"Let's go!" Deitrick exclaims.

"Okay, Deitrick, hang on. We are going to see the baby chicks next, but first I need to check the hydrant." I pull the wagon to the hydrant and see that it is off. I pull the handle into the up position and hear the hose that goes to the hogs fill with water.

"What are you guys doing? I said we were going to see the chicks." Deitrick was already out of the wagon and Rhys was half out.

"What are you doing, Daddy?" Deitrick asks.

"I needed to turn on the water for the hogs. Your uncles turned it off for some reason and forgot to turn it back on. Do you want to go see the chicks or not?" I ask rhetorically.

The boys start to climb back in the wagon. "No, let's go. You can walk. It's just over there."

I pull Charley alone in the wagon, which is much easier than pulling all three kids, and the boys take off knowing where to go.

As we get to the brooder, a protected structure with controlled heating, I collect Rhys and Deitrick. "Hey boys, remember to be very careful in here. You don't want to step on any chicks, do you?"

"I'll be careful." They each reply. Deitrick has wavy hair that goes every which way. If there is a puddle along the way, he'll make sure to cross through it, and he likes to explore by doing. Rhys has straight hair and loves to ask "Why, Daddy?" He's a little more cautious and tends to use his brother as the guinea pig.

Deitrick takes off, pellmell. That kid is so awkward in his movement. He's constantly bumping into things and falling down.

"Don't run, either," I remind them.

As I begin filling the feeders, Rhys and Deitrick follow behind, playing in the feed. They like to pull feed out of the feeders onto the ground, and then pull grit out if its compartment and into the food. I left Charley on the ground next to the doorway, so she can see us. There are plenty of things she can play with on the ground and she seems entertained.

"Remember, boys, Daddy doesn't like messes."

"I know, Dad," Deitrick replies.

"Well, what's this?" I point to the feed scattered on the floor.

Deitrick begins picking the feed and bedding, putting it back in the feeder.

"Thank you, Deitrick. Do you want to help Daddy fill the waterers?"

"Yeah!" Deitrick exclaims.

"Me, too, Dad" Rhys echos.

I set up the three-and-a-half-gallon chick waterers. They are white plastic domes with red plastic bases that screw on. The boys each want to be the one to hold the hose as the water fills. I tell the boys, "You will have to share. Deitrick can go first. Don't get your sister wet."

It takes both hands for Deitrick to squeeze the nozzle on the end of the hose. They both do a remarkably excellent job for being just shy of three-years-old and while they work on that, I carry full waterers back into the brooder.

It doesn't take long for them to get bored and disappear.

"Rhys! Deitrick!" I yell as I try to track them down. I walk around the corner of the barn and see they are playing on a yard tractor that I haven't used in two years. It's okay with me, and they are entertained, so I leave them while I finish with the chicks.

"Hey Charley, how are you doing?" I ask her. She stops crying. She didn't like being left alone. I button up the brooder and reach down to pick up Charley.

"Man, you are a mess. Guess that's what I get for setting you down on the ground. Let's go get your brothers." I tell her as I set her in the wagon. Her pink pants are now brown. Hopefully Krystyl won't be upset if the stains don't come out.

I pull the wagon around the barn. "Okay, boys, let's go back across the street. Do you want to walk or ride in the wagon?"

Rhys replies first, "I want to ride in the wagon."

"I'll walk daddy!" Deitrick shouts.

After I get Rhys settled, we head around the lot.

"Deitrick!" I holler. "Wait for me!" He comes back to me. He is fast when he wants to be.

"Hold my hand," I say. "Now look left, and then…"

"No cars" Deitrick interrupts.

"…right. Deitrick, we still must look and listen for cars. The road is dangerous." There is a car coming from the north about a quarter mile away.

"Car coming, Daddy!" Rhys exclaims from the wagon. He's so excited to have spotted one he nearly jumps out of his seat.

"I see it, son. We'll wait for it to pass." I reply.

After the car passes, Deitrick holds my hand as we cross until we get nearer to the house and then takes off down the hill to the north of the house out into the field where we have the layer hens. Their triangular shelter sits in the field like a gigantic, protective mother hen. Cameron comes out in the truck to help me with chores and plops his wide-brimmed hat on Deitrick's head. Deitrick is in heaven; he loves walking through the hens to collect eggs and spill feed everywhere. Rhys is a little more hesitant so he doesn't wander through the fenced-in area as freely as his brother. Cameron lifts Charley out of the wagon to help her feel included in the action. I spot our one black chicken who lays green eggs and smile. We have come a long way from that winter when the coop burned down.

Once the hens are cared for, we hop in the truck to go out to the cows and broilers. We have six shelters for broilers with one or two shelters for each age-group of chicks. In the early summer, we get chicks practically every week and at our height, we will have twelve or so shelters in the field, each containing about a hundred chickens. Krystyl says the full grown chickens are ugly, but I don't think they look so bad. These ones here are strong and healthy. This is going to be a banner year for chicken on this farm, especially with our two new markets in Meridian and Bay City.

We move on to the cows. Deitrick is most excited about the cows, even though he has to wait on the other side of the fence while I move them. I started out with some Holstein feeders when I first moved to the farm, but when I went to the pasture-based system, I bought six Hereford heifers in 2010, and they have been great mamas for me. Holsteins are the race car breed of milk production with large frames. They don't work well in a pasture based system and wanted to get a more hardy beef breed. We still have two of them, and they give me calves every year. Since that first year with the Herefords, my herd has grown to around fifty head. I can't grow them fast enough to keep up with the demand for our beef. I'm so glad I chose this pasture-based method to raise the cows.

They are so happy when we move them. One even occasionally lets Cameron pet him. Someday it'll be Deitrick or Rhys or Charley out here petting the cows.

It does slow me down, pulling the kids around, and when I'm in the moment it can be frustrating. When I am working on something that takes the majority of my attention, the kids get more freedom. This includes stepping on each other or making a mess of the chicken feed. It also includes locking the truck, turning on the blinkers, climbing on the cab of the truck. Looking back on these moments,though, fills me with joy. My only hope is that my frustrations during the moment don't cause my kids to not want to participate in the future as farmers themselves.

My grandpa, Bud, told me when we had the boys: "Having kids around makes it all worthwhile." Before my children were born, I would not have been able to relate to that statement. Now though, I fully understand what he means. I really didn't develop my community-and-culture-around-food focus until after I had children, and it is through them this vision has been nurtured and developed.

My vision of community and culture around great food brings me hope, too. I want to see that dream become a reality and I need you, the reader, to want it too. Come visit the farm and attend our events. We have them listed on our website gccorganics.com. To create this community, it takes you to participate. Leave the confines of your house and make a drive over to the farm. We'll have great food and amazing environments. We'll have insightful conversations, too. It would be truly special to leave that legacy to the next generation. Imagine all our kids, or our grandkids being able to enjoy each other's company, focused around amazing food and the back-to-the-farm environment. I've seen a glimpse of this environment at our own familial gatherings, and I want to share a similar feeling with you.

When Charlotte turned one in July, we throw a party for her.
My day begins like it does most mornings, with chores. The
house needs to be picked up, but I mainly stick to outside duties,
finishing chores around 10:00. I then clean up the yard around
the house, garage, and woodshed. Our parties usually end in the
back yard around a rectangular fire pit, but they begin in the
front yard. This location is relatively new for parties, but it does
make for beautiful afternoon events in the sun. Our front yard
features two giant oak trees on the west side of the house. Doug,
my father-in-law, and I spend the mid-afternoon mowing the yard
and setting up tables and chairs for our guests.

Since getting into food production, I have insisted on providing
food for events we are either attending or hosting, and today is
no exception. Today, I plan to grill chicken, a staple at our parties,
some pork sausages, and a special treat, brisket. The brisket I will
save for the late party after most people have left. I wrap it in foil
after smothering it with seasoning. It will slow cook on the grill
for four hours before being opened. I am especially excited for
this offering.

While I love to have people over to share good food on the farm,
my introverted nature still kicks in. I tend to hide behind my
cooking, and people who want to talk to me will seek me out to do
so. My favorite part of these gathering is when I see the smiles on
faces because what I have served was delicious, and we all know
this food is the best raised and most nutritious food available.

As family and friends arrive, I have my brothers Cameron, Davis,
and Brandon take the tractor to hook onto a hay wagon and line
a row of bales on it for seats. We will be taking a small tour of the
farm, and so that the hay isn't too uncomfortable, we cover the
bales with sheets. I meet the guests, more warmly with the people
I know.  I just nod and smile toward the guests I don't know. I
hope it's a smile, anyway. After everyone has arrived, I drive the
tractor pulling everyone along for the hay ride. I am careful not

go too fast. The grounds can be rough, and I need to make sure the riders are safe.

I enjoy showing people around. We drive out to see the broilers in the portable shelters and the cows in their daily paddocks. I hear Doug telling them about the operation and lamenting the work. He tells them how much fun he has showing families around the farm and interacting with the animals. We don't run a petting zoo, but we allow people the opportunity to experience a little of the farm life.

There are around fifteen people on the wagon as we swing back around. Family friends with their kids, Rhys, Deitrick, Charlotte, grandparents, and mommy just to name a few. We decide we should drive down to the hogs, too, so that our guests can see them. They are about a mile away under our oak trees. As we pull next to the hog area, the hogs run to us, oinking along the way. It is a delight to watch them come up, excited to see something new. Doug points out how the hogs have rooted up the ground under the trees looking for acorns and grubs, strengthening the existing forest. I decide to ride the wagon back home and have my brother, Cameron, drive us the mile back up to the house.

*Wagon Tour*

When we are back at the house, I go back to the grill, which is in the backyard, to collect the chicken and sausages. I bring them to the front, and everyone says they are hungry. Soon the crowd is relatively quiet as everyone eats. I make sure everyone is satisfied before I sit down to eat while Krystyl is bringing out the cake and ice cream.

We sing "Happy Bithday" to Charley and divvy up the cake. After Charlotte has opened her presents, with her brothers' help, the party starts to thin out. Most people have other obligations and concerns to attend to for the evening, or kids who need to get home for bath-time. A few people stay behind on this Saturday evening, mostly close friends and family.

*Delbert holding Charlotte on her birthday.*

Doug gets a bonfire going in the backyard while my brothers and I pick up the front yard tables and chairs. Krystyl and Grandma Jenny are taking care of the kids, getting them cleaned up from the days events. The kids come out soon after, and we keep a close eye on them around the fire. As we set up a semicircle of chairs around the fire, the remaining guests find a seat. It is nice to hear the stories and the laughter. I pick up Charley and sit down with her.

"Happy birthday, sweetheart. You are one year old." I tell her, showing her one finger.

She doesn't have much to say. She rests her head on my shoulder with her little arms wrapped around me. Charlotte gives me a smile, making my heart swell. As I watch the flames, conversations go on around me, some involving me and some not. That is okay though, I never wanted to be the center of attention and don't need to be, to be happy.

Here is a simple event. I believe it should occur on a regular basis across America because that is what a community used to be based around: healthy food, a safe environment, and good people. Our communities have changed, our food has changed, and our environments have changed. In some respects, for the better, no doubt, but they have come at a cost.

Grabbing even a little bit of that culture and community back from history will also come at a cost. In an era when there doesn't appear to be any time available, we would need to make time. The food we raise isn't the cheapest food either, and for good reasons. I can provide a safe and real environment, though, and I provide the food. I just need good people to bring the conversation and devote the time to developing relationships. Simple conversations about families and about life, and complex conversations about politics or pop culture.

Hope..., we need to have it for the future and for the present. My hope is for the children, yours and mine. We must secure their future by securing their present. Will and determination don't make love—but they help keep it, just as will and determination made this farm but only love can keep it. My hope is that love will keep this farm not only for my benefit but yours as well. Thank you for following me on this journey. Visit us online at gccorganics.com, FaceBook, Pinterest, Twitter, or Instagram. Attend our events, and see us at our markets. I look forward to seeing you soon!

# ACKNOWLEDGEMENTS

The society and culture needed to publish a work is somewhat overwhelming, and it all begins with support from the home. I thank my wife, Krystyl, for the countless hours she put in to get this book to print. It would have been impossible to give the time necessary if I also didn't have my mother-in-law, Jennifer, here to run the household and watch my children, Deitrick, Rhys and Charlotte. Thank you! To my father-in-law, Doug, my brother, Davis, and my employee, Jordan, I am so blessed to have you around to help ensure the farm persists (and sells products) while I devote so much time to other pursuits. My mom, thank you for your support and help, from the moment I was born to now, you've been here for me, and you have made this process a little easier. Ariana Anderson, my friend, thank you for those final edits. Finally, to my grandpa and grandma, Charles (Bud) and Mina, thank you for giving me the opportunity to pursue this career. It hasn't been easy, but the great things in life aren't. Every one of you are my rock, and I love you!

Another piece of this society starts with the insiders. It begins with the New Degree Press, thank you. These people know what it takes to get a book published. Thank you to Michael Pisani, for your support, patience and assistance. To Eric Koester, for your persistence, to Brian Bies, for your cover insight, thank you. Anastasia Armendariz, I loved your vision in making this manuscript flow and allowing for the possibility of fundamental change. Thank you!